THE
UNKNOWN
CHAMPION

THE

FROM FANTASY FOOTBALL
★ ★ ★ ★ ★ ★ ★ ★ ★ ★

UNKNOWN

TO THE TOUCHLINE
★ ★ ★ ★ ★ ★ ★ ★ ★ ★

CHAMPION

A REAL LIFE STORY

RUI MARQUES

First published by Pitch Publishing, 2019

Pitch Publishing
A2 Yeoman Gate
Yeoman Way
Worthing
Sussex
BN13 3QZ
www.pitchpublishing.co.uk
info@pitchpublishing.co.uk

© 2019, Rui Marques

ISBN 978 1 78531 504 6

Typesetting and origination by Pitch Publishing

Printed and bound in India by Replika Press Pvt. Ltd.

Contents

I dedicate this book to the late **Freddie Mercury**, my favourite singer of all time and a permanent spiritual presence, and **Nigel Mansell**, my first idol, a hero for me and a person I identify with in terms of principles.

My wife Patricia was fundamental to my success because of the balance, support and love she gives me, in the good and bad moments.

PART I:
BASES AND ROOTS

PROLOGUE

14 September 2017

It's four in the morning and I'm lying in my bed thinking about the trip that I will start in a few hours, which could be very important to me. For the first time I'm not going to be alone on my trip to Kansas City, as my wife Patricia and my son Leonardo will be travelling with me. I will be there to watch a cup final – the US Open Cup 2017 – between my club Sporting Kansas City and the New York Red Bulls. Lots of questions fill my mind: Will we win the cup? If we lose the match, how should I deal with it? And perhaps most importantly, am I asking too much from my wife and little son by taking them on this long trip? For all these questions, the only certainty I have is that with my family around I feel more confident and happy. And because this could be a really amazing moment, I want to be close to the people who matter most to me.

There is a high probability that two of the players I recommended to the club could play a fundamental role in this game: Gerso Fernandes and Diego Rubio. There is also still a small probability that a third player, Kevin Oliveira, could play. Despite living in Portugal, I feel like I'm part of the group and I contribute to making the team better every day. I have to be positive, I must have a winning mentality, and I believe we will win.

I think back over the 38 years of my life so far and I have more questions: Who would have thought an ordinary guy who loved to play fantasy football competitions would be a scout for a team one step away from winning the US Open Cup? Was this young man with a boring career in the financial world about to find true happiness? And am I building a life story that is interesting enough to write a book about?

1

WHY AM I TELLING MY STORY?

Nowadays anyone can write a book. Just go to a bookstore, have a look at what has already been written and you can write a successful book. But there are countless examples of books that offer nothing of interest or anything new to the reader. There are many books on the shelves about people who have become celebrities without any real talent, and they don't have anything interesting to tell, but there are also books written by quality writers, those who are truly gifted, who have become famous and have built a reputation for creating magnificent tales of fiction or writing their own exciting life stories, which we all love to read. I'm not a celebrity, but I have a great story to tell that's not the result of my imagination, it's real! So, why not? I don't need to create a storyline or use my imagination for anything. My challenge is to write well and tell you what happened to me, hopefully expressing the emotions I felt as best I can. I have decided to tell my story because I think it's something special, unique. I didn't need favours nor did I rely on luck, I was able to win because of my talent and hard work. There were times during the writing of this book that I thought of giving up because I didn't think I'd really triumphed or that I could provide great moments of interest to the reader. But in the end I decided that my story might be interesting enough to keep the reader reading. If characters of fiction can become idols, even though their characteristics and actions are not real, then hopefully my true story can be of interest. If I can inspire or make someone happy, I'll be glad.

I have a good educational background, I was taught to have good principles and values, and have never underestimated the importance of hard work. Like the vast majority of people of my generation in my home country (I have lived in Portugal since I was born in 1979), I was told by my parents that I should focus on studying to earn a college degree so that I would be successful in life. That was great motivation during my childhood and teenage years, so I was a good student, got good grades and went to university.

Unfortunately, when I was ready to enter the working world, I began to realise that not only was my degree (in economics) not enough to guarantee a job, but also that I would not be able to make a difference working in this area. Why did I think this? The simple answer is because I had no passion for finance or any of the subjects that surround it. Working in this field would not bring out the best in me, so I would never really achieve great results. I tried to fool myself for a while, to be honest, and I was not a strong enough person to question whether the path that my parents had recommended to me was the right one for me. Luckily, fate was on my side and I found my way to a better career and future for me. It was maybe a little late, as I was in my mid-twenties by the time I realised, but it was still well in time to pursue my new goals. There are people who know from childhood what they want to be in life, while others spend their lives looking for something and never find it. Now I consider myself to be one of the lucky ones.

I've always loved football, and also competition, so the perfect match for me was fantasy football – a competition in which participants act like coaches and build teams based on the available players from a given league and score points according to the performance of their players. I can recall my earliest memory of football and I know where and when it was: I was listening to the report of a match on my father's car radio when Portugal won against the Soviet Union back in November 1983 and qualified for Euro '84. However, despite the strong connection I've had with football since then, I could never have imagined the happiness that this sport would bring me in the future. The title of this book is *The Unknown Champion* because I managed, against the odds, to win in fantasy football competitions, which were my showcase, then someone gave me an opportunity in the football industry. In this competitive world I've managed to keep on winning, but still nobody knows who I am. Today, I can say that I was the first person (and probably the only one so far) to win the top prize in fantasy football competitions in two different countries, England and Germany. Within three years, I won 'You The Manager' in the *Daily Mirror* in England in 2009/10 and the 'Super Manager' competition in the *Bild* newspaper in Germany in 2012/13. These and other victories are detailed in this book.

In the summer of 2013, after winning the German competition, I started to believe I could achieve my goal of working for a professional football club. Today, more than five years later, I am in my sixth season as a talent scout, working firstly with Estoril Praia from Portugal for two years, then I worked for Sporting Kansas City for three and a half years, an American team in MLS. Both clubs have already signed players recommended by me, and these players have been successful. Now I am starting a new challenge with Legia Warsaw, the current Polish champions. Although I continue to work in the financial sector in a full-time job, I manage my time carefully so I can be successful in both fields. My goal is to work just in football, and every day I take another step towards this. So, this book will also provide details of my scouting career so far.

People who might be interested in reading this book are not necessarily football lovers. If you are interested in fantasy football or scouting then this book could be a good reference for the future. The purpose of the book is not to give tips to succeed in these areas, but I will detail those things that have led to my success, so there will be some wisdom and knowledge. But anyone who appreciates a good story based on willpower, intuition and discipline should enjoy reading this book.

2
FOOTBALL AND ME

During my childhood I experienced some very strong emotions thanks to football, and most of it was positive. This book does not detail every flashback from my first football memories and experiences, but some of them are important because it is likely that they were the basis of the success that I experienced decades later.

I was always fascinated by the play-by-play live football reports on the radio. I remember going on Sunday walks with my grandparents and always taking a small blue radio with me. Sometimes I glued it to my ear, literally. It was my way of following all the action and hearing all the goals scored each afternoon, in a time when all the matches used to be played simultaneously. I loved to memorise the team line-ups and I would repeat them to myself as if I were singing a song. Although my Grandfather Adão was a Sporting Lisbon supporter, I began to develop affection for their rival team – Benfica. This may have been the influence of a neighbour of my grandparents, who was truly passionate about football and Benfica, but also because I was born in the borough of S. Domingos de Benfica, close to the stadium.

I clearly remember learning in March 1984 that football can be so cruel; I had such great expectations watching a European Cup (today the Champions League) match between Benfica and Liverpool. I started to watch the game on TV, but Liverpool scored early on. Then they added a second goal and continued to annihilate my beloved team! My parents convinced me to go to bed and I followed their advice, knowing that Benfica would lose the game for sure. The next day I found that, no surprise, 4-1 had been the final result. The following season, Benfica played Liverpool again and were again knocked out. I developed respect and fear for The Reds. I don't want to be unfair to the other players, but the ones I feared the most and considered the most charismatic were Ian Rush – the elegant striker – and Bruce Grobbelaar – a funny goalkeeper.

Another defeat I found tough was a game in which Benfica were crushed by arch rivals Sporting in December 1986. As usual, I was listening to the match live on the radio and it seemed so surreal. When Sporting scored the fifth goal to take a 5-1 lead, I begged my mum to turn off the radio. The final result was 7-1, and I couldn't believe a score like that had happened. I didn't cry that day, but months later I remember tears falling from my face after a home defeat versus a team called Marítimo. It's weird when I look back now and remember my behaviour and emotional reactions to defeats; the majority of children my age (seven or eight years old) probably wouldn't react the same way, but for me I really felt the pain in my soul. I was already a competitive person and had a real desire to win, and my will was embodied in the Benfica team. The first time I went to the Stadium of Light was in January 1988 to see Benfica versus Belenenses. I was with my father, who likes football, but he's not passionate about it. Our seats were right at the top and when I saw the whole stadium for the first time, and its beautiful green pitch, I thought it was magnificent, like I was seeing a perfect piece of art. Benfica won 2-0 and I was captivated by every part of a live football match.

I was lucky to grow up in an era when Portuguese football was going through an excellent period in the 1980s. Our national team qualified for two major tournaments, Euro '84 and World Cup '86. Portugal did very well in Europe, only losing to the host country, France, in the semis after an epic match that was decided during extra time. The Mexico '86 tournament was the first World Cup I watched (I was two years old during the 1982 World Cup and I don't remember any of it). My greatest memories were, of course, Diego Maradona's performances and the way he led Argentina to victory. Portugal lost to Morocco 1-3 and left the tournament on a low note. In club terms, FC Porto had a golden period, winning the European Cup in 1987 against Bayern Munich in a match that I thoroughly enjoyed watching. It was a pleasure to see Rabah Madjer's famous goal off the back heel. I also got up in the middle of the night to watch FC Porto play and win the 1987 Intercontinental Cup match against Peñarol from Uruguay on a snowy pitch. Benfica also clinched two European Cup finals in 1988 and 1990, losing both. My passion for football was confirmed in those years, in such a way that it would never disappear.

I have such great memories of completing my football sticker albums back then. My grandmother, Joana, told me that I was given my first sticker album in around 1982 and after that I became obsessive about collecting them. When the album was from a major tournament I enjoyed it even more because I could collect stickers of great players from all over the world, from Brazil to Cameroon, never forgetting the ever-present South Korea. When I turned 18, before the France '98 World Cup, I lost my motivation and that was the first one I didn't finish, but I started collecting again with my son for the Russia 2018 World Cup collection and I really enjoyed it. Some years ago, I bought a set of all the sticker albums from the Euros and World Cups between 1970 and 2006 and I consider this to be one of my most precious possessions.

During my teenage years, I think my all-time favourite football player, who became my idol, was Alan Shearer, an English striker who dominated the Premier League top scorer charts in the mid-90s and was the Euro '96 top scorer. I wanted to be like him because he was a centre-forward – the position I liked to play the most – and I identified with the way he played. He was intelligent and had the ability to understand where to position himself, predicting the way the play would develop. His tremendous finishing skills made him so effective, and when fit he would score amazing goals and he had a fantastic goal-per-game ratio. He was also a special player because of his strong principles during his career. He declined proposals from better teams to stay at his childhood club – Newcastle United. However, his peak was at Blackburn Rovers where he won the Premier League title in the 1994/95 season. He doesn't have many titles on his CV, but individually he broke many records with his consistent performances throughout his entire career.

As well as watching football, I also liked to play it. I usually played as a forward and had the job of getting in to the best position I could to score goals. I remember in elementary school I was considered to be one of the best players in my class. In 1988 my mother enrolled me in a small club in the city where I lived, Estrela da Amadora.

The team had won the championship in my age category the previous season. The first training sessions went really well and I excelled, scoring many goals. However, the coach criticised me, saying I didn't run as much as the others. It was true, but I was trying to stay in the right place so I could score when I got the chance – and I scored a lot of goals, guessing the play and positioning myself in the right spot. I was a bit demoralised, lost confidence and, because I was only young, I started asking to play as a right-winger in the training sessions, like my favourite player at the time – a Benfica player called Pacheco, who was actually a left-winger but as I was not a leftie I had to play on the right wing. I was only nine years old and my natural position was as a central forward, so it didn't really work for me. It would have been very helpful to have had an adult on my side, who could have given me advice and guidance. But I can't use that as an excuse, many young people have had the strength to succeed playing in far more difficult circumstances than me.

I never tried again, probably because of instability in my family (my parents were about to divorce) or because I was constantly being told by my mother that studies should be my only priority. I remember when I was 17 years old I entered a five-a-side tournament and she told me that I shouldn't play because I could 'break a leg' and wouldn't be able to go to college. Coincidence or not, I ended up twisting my left foot in one of the matches, but it was nothing serious so I managed to get into college later that year, in 1997. Two years later, I managed to win a soccer championship, also five-a-side but this time indoor, with my class team – I scored a few goals and got a medal for it. I have good memories of great wins and performances in games with colleagues and friends. I think I had the talent and mentality to be a professional football player, and I will always be a bit frustrated that I never made it and I didn't really fight for it. I will not pressure my son to be a football player, but, I can't lie, I'd be really happy if he built a career in the beautiful game.

3
FANTASY FOOTBALL – THE BEGINNING

In the summer of 1995 a new concept emerged in Portugal, a game organised by a sports newspaper, *Record*, called 'Liga Fantástica' – the first fantasy football competition launched in my home country. Nobody in Portugal had heard of this type of competition, but it was already very popular in countries like England and the USA. I remember seeing the contest logo published on the cover of the newspaper and I was curious to see what it was, but when I read the terms and conditions it didn't appeal to me. Despite the possibility of being a virtual coach, choosing the players from the Portuguese league, there was one part of it that seemed quite archaic and put me off doing it: the team management would be done by post. We had to send letters to make the substitutions we wanted, which would mean a lot of time lost before the changes became effective, so I decided not to enter. When college began again that year, two of my closest colleagues asked me if I had seen the new competition in the *Record* newspaper. I said yes, but I was not playing. They were incredulous because they knew me very well and thought the game was made for me, and they had been excited to talk to me about it. It's quite interesting that I still remember this conversation and their reactions, even though I completely lost contact with them. Neither of them will know how important fantasy football became to me. But I must say that their intuition was indeed spot on.

The next season I entered a team. The management was now being done by phone, but the phone calls to change the team or to find out the overall leader board positions were quite expensive. My results were nothing special. The following season, my enthusiasm grew a little, but I didn't take it seriously, and I ended up picking my favourite players, not applying any strategy or devoting enough time and energy to get results. I didn't pick the best players from FC Porto or Sporting either because I didn't want to watch their games – my love of Benfica was doing me some damage!

But around the middle of the 2000/01 season the 'click' happened. Teams could be managed online, which was a much more efficient way of managing your team. The prizes were quite attractive and were paid in gold bars, too. I was 21 years old by then and I was smarter than I had been. I knew I had to set better goals and decide my priorities in life. I had a stable relationship with Patricia, and I was well placed to finish my degree the next year. I was not the Benfica-crazy supporter that I had been before, and that would really help me in my first success in fantasy football. In January 2001 I decided to make an investment (for a student with no fixed income it was a big and risky investment, the equivalent of £35 nowadays) and I bought 18 magazines, as each one had an application form to enter the competition, which meant I was going to have 18 teams to manage plus the other team that I had already registered at the beginning of the season. After reading an article about one of the weekly winners and having analysed their winning team, I had an idea for a strategy that would give me a good chance of winning the weekly prize, which was equivalent to £2,300 in gold bars – very attractive. My strategy was to have a defensive block from each of the 18 teams that played in the Portuguese league at the time in each of my 19 teams. I still had an extra team so I could repeat one of the blocks and then also change the midfielders or the forwards. It was not exactly a revolutionary or innovative strategy, as I noticed that other competitors were doing the same, but if, during a weekend, a team clinched a win without conceding a goal, and I had the best midfielders and attackers of the week, that would make a difference and I would be in front and a candidate for winning the weekly prize. I made a wise decision to always have a defensive block from each team, and even when a weaker team played a top team, I would still bet on a surprise and build a block from the underdog.

The rules of the game were basically the same as any fantasy football competition, but there are always some aspects that are slightly different across the different competitions. In this case, I remember each player had a price that could rise or drop from week to week and we had a total budget limit for the 11 players and also for a coach. We could opt for different tactics (change from a 3-5-2 to a 5-4-1, for example) and there were no limits on the number of players that you could select per club. There were other details that had to be taken into account too, such as the mandatory choice of a Portuguese player playing abroad, a bit of a joker. The budget was pretty tight; I had to choose cheaper players so I could still buy the top players, which is one of the common difficulties of this type of game. The points scored were based on the performance of the player, evaluated by the journalists, plus bonus points for each goal or clean sheet for goalkeepers/defenders/midfielders. The coach scored the same points as the players in his team earned each match.

The results came quickly for me, less than three months after starting to play with this strategy. In the first week of April in 2001, I had an excellent score. A defensive block from one of the average teams from the Portuguese league, Farense (the team from Faro, Algarve, the capital in the south of Portugal), who won 2-0 that weekend, meant that my team scored a good number of defensive bonus points. Added to this, I had a powerful combination in the midfield and attack with players from FC Porto and SC Braga, who were good scorers that weekend. I thought I could have a team with enough points to win it. When I went to buy the newspaper on Tuesday morning, the day the results were published, I was anxious and had high hopes of being the winner. But I didn't win, I finished in third place, just one point behind the leader. I felt some disappointment after being so close, but it showed me that I was on the right track. My strategy was good, and I was good enough to make it work because my knowledge of Portuguese football was excellent and I had enough analytical power to pick the best players based on their prices. The following day the results of a parallel competition were published – the prize was a mobile phone donated by a communications company who were the main sponsor of the game – and I was the winner because I had the highest score among the Benfica supporters! So, less than three months after my initial investment I won my first prize, a small one but still notable. I was really motivated after that, and I knew I could do better. From then on in my less interesting college classes I was usually writing players' names in my notebook and planning possible teams for the weekend!

The first great moment of my fantasy football career was in May 2001. That weekend Benfica played Alverca – a team who had only been in the Portuguese top flight for a short time – and, applying my strategy, one of my fantasy teams was based on the Alverca defensive block. They were less powerful and were far from favourites, but in football you never know when a surprise is around the corner. The final result was Benfica 0 Alverca 2 – in the Stadium of Light! Ironically, I couldn't build a defensive block exactly the same as the Alverca team because there were doubts about who would play in each position of the defence and some players were playing as defenders but listed as midfielders. Only goalkeeper Paulo Santos and defender Ricardo Carvalho were certain choices in the defensive block (curiously two players who reached international level in the future, with Ricardo Carvalho becoming a key player for Chelsea a year later). So, my solution was to create a core structure of Alverca players in my team because I suspected that, if they won, all the players would get a good review from the journalists. This turned out to be a key factor in scoring as many points as possible. So, I chose a central midfielder and attacking midfielder from Alverca, and Pedro Mantorras, a promising young Angolan player, as the central forward. The coach I chose was also from Alverca, Jesualdo Ferreira, who got the maximum score of three points as his team won. With five Alverca players plus the coach, I had another six players to choose. But one of them was a given, Fernando Couto from Lazio Rome, because we had to choose a Portuguese player who was playing abroad when we registered the team and you weren't allowed to replace him. Unfortunately, he was suspended for doping (Nandrolone – a substance that was found in some players at the time) and so I got negative points because he did not play – one point was deducted if a player was not taking part in the game. But the more popular Portuguese players in foreign teams, like Luís Figo or Rui Costa, didn't do very well that week, losing both their matches, so it was not a deal breaker. One of the other five players I chose was Barroso, the Braga midfielder, who was very dangerous when taking direct free kicks, and at the weekend he scored another brilliant goal. The remaining four were two pairs of players from Boavista – Frechaut and Jorge Couto – and FC Porto – Clayton and Pena. All these players performed above average that weekend, scoring goals or getting high ratings. The tactical system I chose was a 3-5-2 because I thought it would suit the core Alverca team better.

On Sunday evening, with all the matches played, I thought I had a good chance of winning. But with hundreds of thousands of participants, you can never take anything for granted. On Monday night, at around 9pm, I got a call from *Record*! Yes, it was confirmation of my victory. The feeling was amazing, difficult to describe, but certainly one of the best feelings in life.

I felt like a champion – probably for the first time as an adult. To me, I had done something special, and in my head I could hear one of my all-time favourite songs by Queen – 'We Are The Champions'. Since I was 12 years old, I have been a huge fan of Freddie Mercury and his band – sadly Freddie died in 1991 before I had the chance to see a live performance. But I lived my teenage years buying all their albums and enjoying their music from the 70s and 80s, and now I could really feel the meaning of the song because I was finally a champion.

Achieving something when the odds are against you, and when the result is because of hard work, is fantastic and it made me so happy. You always need a little bit of luck, though – I scored 69 points just like another competitor, but the tie-breaker was the budget, and as my team was of a lower value I was declared the winner. On the call, the journalist interviewed me for the newspaper, and they told me that a photographer would meet me and take a picture of me holding the *Record* newspaper. I felt important for the first time in my life. It's funny that I didn't win with my pure strategy idea, but I was able to adapt quickly and efficiently, well aware of the limiting factor of the Alverca defensive structure. Luck came my way and rewarded my ability to improvise and be creative.

On the following Wednesday, the article was printed in the newspaper. It's not the best picture of me, but there was a whole page dedicated to my victory in one of the biggest Portuguese newspapers. The title was 'I avoided selecting Benfica players' and the subtitle was 'Rui set aside club preferences and wins the prize'. I was always a strong Benfica supporter, but ironically I was now reaching my most glorious moment in football with their defeat. On that day, I also learned that I had won the sponsor's prize again, another cell phone. Two months later I went to the *Record* headquarters to collect my prize – 240 grams of gold bars that totalled around £2,300 at the gold rate at that time. I kept the bars hidden until I sold them, and I bought a laptop with most of the money.

The following season, I kept the same strategy to try and win the weekly prizes. I still didn't feel capable of the consistency required to fight for the monthly or annual prizes. If you compare me to a runner, I was a sprinter in my early days, but as you will see I became a marathon runner later in my fantasy football career.

I had a great start to the season. On the third match day, I reached seventh place, and by the end of September I thought another win was on the cards. I built a team based on the Boavista defence and my two strikers both scored hat-tricks, and one of them was not exactly a popular choice. In terms of probability, I thought I was more likely to win now than when I won in May. But on Monday night I didn't get the phone call. When I bought the newspaper on Tuesday, the result was difficult to swallow – second place. I was quite frustrated, and I had a spell of poor results after that. I finished the season without winning any prizes. In the 2002 World Cup, knock-out phase, I finished an honourable fourth, but in a somewhat childish and immature manner I decided to temporarily retire from fantasy football, and I tried other things to have fun and earn money.

4

TROUBLED YEARS

In the summer of 2002 I discovered a new hobby and lost interest in fantasy football competitions. I've always been savvy when it comes to exploring the potential of the internet, and I started online betting. My bets were basically on tennis (another sport that I enjoy) and football. I shifted my commitment to studying this new activity.

At the same time, I started a new chapter in another area of my life – I was now sending out CVs to try and get a job, although at the time I was still missing four mandatory subjects to complete my economics degree. It was a period of my life when I remember being a bit of a drifter. I began to realise that it wouldn't be as easy to get a job as I had imagined. I was spending my time going from interview to interview, facing rejections, and helping in my father's company – although I was working in the distribution and commercial areas of the business, which did not match my newly acquired skills from college. But I made some money and managed to complete some more subjects, and I only had one left to go by the summer of 2003.

As I continued with my online betting, getting more experienced, I started to increase the amounts, taking greater risks, but I couldn't make the kind of profit I would need to be financially secure. In May 2004 I reached over €500 profit, when FC Porto won the Champions League, but then I entered an abysmal phase; for example, I lost a bet on the Roland Garros tennis tournament – the player I bet on to win, Guillermo Coria from Argentina, wasted two match points and ended up losing to Gaston Gaudio, who was also from Argentina but a much worse player. During the 2003/04 season I made some bets against Arsenal when they were playing difficult away matches, after a long streak without defeat, but I lost them all – and that team went on to make history and will be forever known as The Invincibles, the only English team to finish undefeated in the league for more than 100 years – since Preston North End in the 1880s. Was I cursed? In the Euro 2004 competition, which was played in Portugal, I had another disastrous moment when I bet that Portugal would beat Greece in the final and that Portugal forward Pedro Pauleta would score a goal, even though he was yet to score in the tournament, which was really strange as he was the number-one, all-time scorer for Portugal at the time (now it's Cristiano Ronaldo). Many people believed that Portugal would finally win a competition, with Luís Figo or Rui Costa being the 'old' guys and Cristiano Ronaldo, the 'next big thing', mixing the generations. But it was Greece who made the party, winning 1-0, and Pauleta left the tournament without a goal. It was a terrible day for me, perhaps one of the lowest moments of my life. But when you hit the bottom, you have to be smart and realise what you have to change to get back to the top. I started to think that betting wasn't for me. Something always seemed to go wrong, and it didn't feel good when I lost; I couldn't get my head straight afterwards. Sometimes I tried to overcome a lost bet by taking a riskier one to make up for it, which often resulted in a double loss. It was a struggle against myself, and those are the most difficult struggles.

That same month, July 2004, I began to see the light at the end of the tunnel. Through an internet forum that I used, along with other competitors of 'Liga Record', I was made aware of a new fantasy football competition called 'You The Manager' organised by the English newspaper the *Daily Mirror*. The prizes were amazing – the winner of the championship would get £100,000. The timing seemed perfect because coach José Mourinho had just signed for Chelsea, as well as two Portuguese players, Paulo Ferreira and Ricardo Carvalho. I shifted my focus back to fantasy football and gradually abandoned online betting. I saw most of the games at my grandmother Palmira's house, who had kindly signed up for the Portuguese cable channel that broadcast the matches, and she did it without knowing how important it would be for my future. Mourinho and Chelsea won the league at their first attempt, but my first season wasn't quite so impressive!

I managed to achieve some stability in my career from July 2004 to September 2005, working for banks, although it was always on temporary contracts – I was usually working on maternity cover contracts for about four months, so I was still moving from branch to branch. And in the autumn of 2005, things started to improve in my fantasy football. I got my best result so far in 'Manager of the Month', a monthly competition that was part of 'You The Manager', achieving sixth place. In October I was given a job working for a betting company in Gibraltar. I decided to go, but I ended up changing my mind and returning to Portugal because I felt that on a personal level the price was too high – I didn't want to be away from Patricia; we'd been together for more than six years by then and I couldn't imagine my life without. I just wanted to have a proper job and save some money so we could start thinking about getting married. I returned and enrolled back in university to finish my degree and pass econometrics, the one subject I was missing. It was a complicated and turbulent autumn, but I thought it was a good omen that by the new year I would finally be back on track. My favourite song at the time was 'One Way Ticket to Hell ... and Back' from the English band The Darkness, and it described my life at the time. I was trying to get back on track from what seemed to me to be a trend of instability and a waste of my best years.

It was in January 2006 that I finally passed econometrics. But unfortunately to finish the degree I would now have to take some extra subjects because the course program had changed. Nothing could stop me now though, and later that year I finally completed it. I was finally free of the university, which I'm not that proud of having attended now. It is common to hear that university prepares us for life and I tend to agree, but only because it's the first time we come across unscrupulous people who occupy positions without merit. I was taught by many teachers who had no skills to do the job, but I also had many excellent teachers, although I think they were the exception. Anyway, I was now an economics graduate, but honestly nothing changed in terms of my ability to get a job. However, without this weight on my shoulders, by coincidence or not, I started a positive period in my life.

In February 2006 I decided to invest some money, buying new teams in 'You The Manager' to attack the monthly prize, which was £10,000. The results did not go in my favour in the first month, but in March I managed to fight for the victory right to the end. I was quite solid throughout the month, with Cristiano Ronaldo being one of my best players, and I got to the last game in first place. It felt extraordinary to be leading a championship of hundreds of thousands of people with only one game left before it finished. Throughout the season, the competition rules allowed three transfer windows, which meant for most months the teams registered at the beginning of the month would have to be the same until the end, as in this case. The last game was Manchester United against West Ham, and for me to be the winner of the month it would be enough if Manchester United conceded a goal, because the only competitors that could beat me were those with the Manchester United defence block. It didn't happen the way I wanted, as they beat West Ham 1-0 with a Ruud van Nistelrooy goal and I ended up in sixth place. I felt like a loser, so close to victory, but I was on the right track and reaching new highs in my fantasy football career. I could only continue working and hope the results would appear, but I'd rather it was sooner than later.

5

FINDING MY WAY

The 2006 World Cup was coming up and Germany would be the host nation for the big tournament. The *Daily Mirror* launched 'You The Manager World Cup', and I decided to play, but I only entered three teams because I didn't have a job and money in the bank was becoming scarcer. It is a quick tournament and you have almost no error margin, otherwise you will have no chance of winning it. I set up my teams based on my analysis and predictions for the tournament. I thought Italy would win but had a hard group (USA, Czech Republic and Ghana) and therefore I had to wait for the right time to use my limited substitutions (ten in the whole tournament) to bring in some Italian players; France would go far guided by Zidane, who had announced that this competition would be his farewell to football; and England would have a solid tournament led by a golden generation of players like Lampard, Gerrard and Beckham. I didn't think the favourites and current champions Brazil would win, despite having Ronaldinho Gaucho in his prime, or that hosts Germany were a candidate, despite playing at home, and I was not confident that Portugal would do well either, maybe because of my Euro 2004 bet trauma. So, France and England were two of my main initial bets, and I added some low-budget players to my team as well – mainly from Switzerland, Sweden and Tunisia – who would only have to score an average number of points to keep me on track.

I was cautious in the group stage and decided to completely avoid substitutions. I had a slow start and my positions after the group stage were nothing special, but I knew my approach was defensive and I hadn't made any significant mistakes, so now I had to be patient and wait for the right moment to attack. When the last 16 had been decided, I analysed the draw and thought Italy had everything they needed to go far. I spent some money on substitutions to build an Italian defensive block in the best of my three teams, and I began to rise up the table as Italy won their matches without conceding any goals, first to Australia, then Ukraine in the quarters. Adding to this, Zambrotta, an Italian defender, scored one of the goals against the Ukrainians and Brazil lost in the quarters against France, just as I predicted. I was not expecting England to be eliminated against Portugal in this round, but it was still OK for me, because, despite having some England players, I still had some substitutions to make. Before the semi-finals I was already in the top 20 and still had a substitution to make. I thought I had an opportunity to win and it was in my control – the substitution I had left had to be the right one.

With France facing Portugal, I decided to 'buy' Zidane for my midfield! In the other game I was hoping that Italy would beat Germany, and if they could do it without conceding any goals that would be perfect. My predictions were correct and France won 1-0, with Zidane scoring from a penalty kick. In the other game, Italy beat Germany 2-0 with a goal from one of my defenders, Grosso! I celebrated this goal like crazy! I was in the top ten with two matches to go.

But to get to the top, I would need something more. In the consolation match, I needed to know who would finish third as I had a player in my team that could make a difference – Bastian Schweinsteiger from Germany – it was likely that no one above me in the table would have him. I wasn't sure if he would play in the game as coaches sometimes change their teams and play the less-used players. The game started and 'Schweini' was in the starting 11. I just wanted him to score, I didn't care if Portugal came third or fourth. Let's not be hypocrites, everybody in my situation would put their individual interest above their country!

I had selected Schweinsteiger because in one of the first games of the tournament I watched him and was sure that he was in good shape, confident with his shooting abilities, and he was trying hard to score, but the shots were just not going in and he hadn't scored in the tournament up to now. It was one of those moments when my intuition was spot on and I made the right decision. I was optimistic and felt a very good positive energy before the game in Sesimbra. Game on: Germany got the first goal and it was scored by Bastian Schweinsteiger! What a great shot from outside the box; I moved into a state of euphoria. Some minutes later he scored another goal, again it was brilliant! And then he made a key contribution (scoring bonus points) to a third goal, an own goal by a Portuguese player who was trying to block another shot from Schweinsteiger. When the game ended, I was looking forward to the update. I couldn't believe it, I was the new leader – first place – and there was only one game left, the big final between Italy and France, which would take place the next day.

I knew my chances were good. I had more players from Italy, but I also had the best player from France, Zidane. I didn't know what my rivals had as their team line-ups were not public. Kick-off, and it's France who score relatively early with a Zidane penalty. I wasn't worried at all, and Italy reacted quickly, equalising with a goal from Materazzi, curiously the only Italian defender I didn't have because Alessandro Nesta was the usual starter, but he was injured. I had Buffon, Zambrotta, Grosso and Cannavaro. Near the end of the game, with the score at 1-1, Zidane was sent off for headbutting Materazzi. I was worried that the negative points I'd get for his sending off would be harmful to my chances, but I tried to remain optimistic. The game went to penalties but they didn't count for scoring purposes. I felt really nervous but I thought I could have won. I tried to relax while waiting for the final results to be updated. Would it be the title of world champion and a cheque for £30,000? No! Another big blow. I was down to third place. The winner had picked Materazzi and overtaken me. He also had Zidane, so it was not his sending off that led to my defeat. I was frustrated again. The winner was an Irish man, the same guy who had won the 'You The Manager' monthly competition in March that year in that last game when I had also been leading. He was a big investor, he always bought a huge number of teams. But with only three teams; I had made it to the end, although I couldn't stay on top, I had been unlucky. I was left with the consolation of a £2,500 cheque, which was still my highest prize so far so I was hopeful for the future. At the time, the pound to euro exchange rate was strong so the amount I received was substantial. Patricia gave me her full support and she believed that I would be successful in the near future. At least the bitter taste of the money lost in the Euro 2004 Final bet had now been erased. Now I had to prepare for the next season, and I was happy that I had achieved another milestone – my first win in an international fantasy football competition.

That year, I started work for a French multinational company in the transportation business. It was a monthly-renewable contract, and I was hired to replace a young guy who had gone abroad to work. I remember my supervisor giving me the tasks that no one else wanted, such as photocopying, but my third place in the World Cup gave me the strength to cope. Then I remember one day I was asked by the manager to undergo some medical tests, which was an excellent sign because it meant that the company were happy with my work and they wanted to check my health before renewing my contract. However, a few days later there was an abrupt twist. I was informed that my contract would not be renewed and I would be dismissed at the end of the month. Later I learned that the guy I had replaced wanted to come back. I also learned that he was the same nationality as one of the directors, Uruguayan. I don't want to be a 'cry baby' and use this book to complain, but this kind of experience shaped my personality and helped me to be stronger and guide me to my wins in the future. I was so innocent back then that I didn't get angry and said a fond farewell to all the people I had worked with. But when I think about it today, more than a decade later, it makes me feel a bit angry.

So, in October 2006, at the age of 27, I was again unemployed and lacking any kind of direction. My marriage plans were again delayed and the pressure was rising. Over the next two months I gave everything I had to finding a new job. I went to all the employment agencies I knew. I walked so much that my leg muscles were as strong as if I was working out in a gym. Finally, I started a work contract in December and this gave me the stability I needed to achieve what I have achieved in my life.

I remember starting the 2006/07 season very well in 'You The Manager', reaching third place in the overall table, but throughout the year I didn't win anything special. I stayed in the top 50 in the 'Manager of the Season' competition, but ironically it was the fantastic rise of Cristiano Ronaldo in that time that destroyed my ambitions. It was a game rule that all the teams should play on 4-3-3 tactical formation. I was more Lampard and Gerrard and saved the other midfield position for a cheaper midfielder, which turned out to be a crucial mistake as Ronaldo was listed as a midfielder and he took Manchester United back to the top that season. Once the season was over and I'd had time to think about it, I came to the conclusion that I was playing with a small number of teams and I had to consider investing more money and time if I wanted to be a real contender for the big titles.

I used to only play the *Daily Mirror* competition but other English newspapers, such as *The Sun* or *Daily Telegraph*, also had fantasy football games, all with hundreds of thousands of participants. The best prizes were all around £100,000, which was really fantastic. I realised that there were people who invested more and more each season, buying hundreds of teams, and that the popularity of this type of game was rising. I was just a small fish in the middle of a great big ocean, and although I had already shown my talent I couldn't compete with competitors who had more resources to buy more teams than me. From Croatians, Bulgarians, Hungarians, Irish and, of course, the English, there were many people around the world who invested heavily and dominated. Having a number of teams was especially helpful at the beginning of the season. When a key player was injured, it meant you could change your players and you would always have some teams without injuries, which made a big difference. I had to consider a higher investment for the next season in August 2007.

I've always been, and I still am, a risk-averse person. I like to think about my decisions and I try to be cautious and balanced. But I really believed in my talent, I thought that I would win with more investment, so why not take this step and risk some money? I was afraid of spending the money right up to the last minute, but I knew that to be competitive and implement a winning strategy I had to buy a higher number of teams. Otherwise the 'sharks' would once again beat me, no matter how hard I tried and how good I was. I would have preferred a fair game, equal to equal, with a defined limit for the numbers of teams registered per person (later in my career I had the chance to participate in a competition in Germany with a rule of a maximum of six teams per person and my results there show that I was a great competitor), but now all I could do was have courage and buy more teams. Patricia supported me unconditionally and even lent me half of the money. I think I bought more than 100 teams, but that number was still less than half what some participants had. However, it gave me the structure I needed to face the big investors. I organised all the information in spreadsheets and implemented my strategy after much study, preparing myself for the best possible start to the championship. I would use some of the teams in monthly winner attempts and others to fight for the 'Manager of the Year award'. I made the mistake of telling some close friends and family that I was dedicating more time and investing more money, and their reactions were pretty negative, saying: 'Rui, take life seriously!' or 'Rui, you will make more money sewing shoes than playing those kind of games.' How happy I am when I remember those words now!

I got an extra boost in the summer of 2007 as I bought the autobiography of my first idol, Nigel Mansell, the Formula One driver. Since I was six years old, I can remember cheering for him in races. After I read the book, I concluded that I have lots of things in common with him regarding principles and attitudes in life, which was fascinating to discover and gave me a lot of strength. I believed in my talent, I had already demonstrated my value, but I needed a more competitive 'car' with a 'good engine' to challenge other competitors. I followed Mansell's career passionately, and I was ecstatic after the well-deserved 1992 title in Formula One and in 1993 in Formula Indy, and I was sad when he lost the championship unfairly in 1986, when I was only seven years old. I went to qualifying sessions for the Portuguese Grand Prix that year wearing a UK flag cap because of him! I considered him to be the best. The history of his career is amazing; he faced many adversities to get to the top and only after reading the book did I understand how tough his path to achieve his goals had been.

In professional terms, I was still in the same job and I thought I should stay there for longer because the management were happy with my work. That gave me some peace of mind and stability. All the pieces of the puzzle were beginning to fit together.

During the pre-season I worked very hard, prepared very well, and tried to get as much information as possible about the friendly matches of all the 20 teams that were taking part in the English Premier League. I had to study all the new players in the league to avoid surprises. I stayed awake until very late some nights, organising the teams in a way that I can only define as 'perfection'. My concentration was very high, it was like studying for an exam, preparing for all the questions that might appear.

Once the competition started in August, teams couldn't be changed until the middle of the following month, when the transfer freeze would be off (I think the maximum number of transfers allowed was 15 at that time). It would require more work and attention, but also reduced the random factor of having players with injuries and not being able to replace them. It was a rule that was in my favour, in my opinion. In August we had to keep the same 11 for the whole month. That meant whoever selected the best 11 players at the beginning of the month would win £10,000. Was this magic combination on my spreadsheets?

PART II:
COMPETITION AND WINNING

6

THE BEST OF ME

Saturday, 11 August 2007

The English football championship began and I went to my in-law's house in Sesimbra with Patricia to spend the weekend there, as usual. I had made my decisions and I was confident I'd done as much as I could. Now, it was time to roll the dice. In addition to competing for the top spots in the 'Manager of the Month', I also wanted to fight for the top prize of 'Manager of the Year'. Whoever won the top spot in August's 'Manager of the Month' would be in the lead overall when transfers were allowed. So, on both fronts, it was crucial to start well.

I felt confident, but having invested a substantial amount of money meant I was under a lot of pressure. In this competition there was a new rule that limited the number of players you could choose per club to three, so if I decided to make a team based, for example, on Chelsea not conceding goals, I would not be able to choose the full defensive block, only the goalkeeper and two defenders (or three defenders). The teams that were expected to fight for victory in the league were Manchester United, Chelsea, Arsenal and Liverpool. Aston Villa, Tottenham and Everton were potential outsiders. Most of my teams followed the model of a goalkeeper and two defenders from each of these teams, which would give me a reasonable defence. It was mandatory to play a 4-3-3 formation, but by applying my strategy of a consistent defence, the remaining budget would allow me to choose three top players for the midfield and attack, with six (3+3) places left. That is to say, I would also have to rely on three players from outsider teams like Bolton, Wigan or Birmingham.

The English league back then featured very consistent midfielders, with Frank Lampard appearing every week. Cristiano Ronaldo played mostly as a winger and was listed as a midfielder, and because of his previous season's achievements he was also an obvious choice. Steven Gerrard also appeared as a very strong candidate. But if I chose these three, there would be no room for top strikers, who would also certainly earn points for my team, such as Didier Drogba, Wayne Rooney or Fernando Torres. I had to find the right balance. This is, in essence, the point of fantasy football, managing the budget in a balanced way and finding the best formula that is as close to perfect as possible to win the game, playing safe with some choices, but taking risks with others.

The largest number of games played simultaneously were usually on Saturday afternoons. When these games began, I felt so much excitement. One of the first goals of the first afternoon was from a Derby County midfielder called Matt Oakley, who I had excluded, despite being on my list of possible choices as a lower-price midfielder. I felt angry, and a negative energy invaded my mind, reminding me of my losses in the recent past. But I managed to suppress this negativity, as I was sure I had made a good decision not including him. I had done my research and the evidence suggested to me that the players I had chosen were better options. At the end of the day, I thought I'd got the balance right, so I was happy. The first update of the table showed that I had done the best in terms of the highest number of well-ranked teams. I was also playing in a competition called 'mini-leagues', where each competitor chose his teams and they could be grouped with other competitors' teams, then the group total was used to determine the ranking in the table. So, when I was leading in this competition it meant I had more teams doing well than anyone else. This was a good indication of how I was doing in the main competition.

On the second day of the competition, there was an event that would have a significant effect on the fantasy football scores: Cristiano Ronaldo was sent off with a straight red! As well as the negative points that I got for this, he was also suspended until the end of the month. This meant that the best team of the month could not have him in it, because the amount he cost to buy meant he needed to earn a high number of points, and that could not happen in August now.

This would surely eliminate all the teams with Cristiano Ronaldo in them. The vast majority of my teams were out because I had picked him, but where I had picked my defensive blocks from the Manchester United team (where, for example, I had goalkeeper Van der Sar, defenders Nemanja Vidic and Patrice Evra), the limit of three players per team had forced me to exclude Ronaldo, and those teams would be in the fight if Manchester United could clinch a good number of 'clean sheets' during the month. This was an interesting situation for me because the teams I had with this structure, using the Manchester United defence, were now very strong.

By the time we reached the final round of matches in the last weekend in August, I was in the running to be a possible winner. Manchester United couldn't concede any goals against Tottenham if I was to stand a chance. Looking at the results so far that month, it was already a good advantage if a team could keep two clean sheets in four matches. If Manchester United kept a clean sheet, the midfield and attacking players' performances would be the deciding factor. There had already been some important contributions in these areas before the last set of matches because all my midfielders and strikers had scored at least one goal, with Chelsea's Lampard and Bolton's Anelka standing out with a terrific number of points. Of course, if a different player had a fantastic game the last weekend of the month, all the scores would be shuffled. But in the end nothing significant happened, so my fate was in the hands of the Manchester United defence.

Sunday, 26 August 2007

Manchester United against Tottenham was the penultimate match of the month. I decided not to follow the game and just check the result at the end. Unlike the scenario in March 2006 when I needed Manchester United to concede a goal to win, now it was the opposite! I felt that this time I had to win, I deserved to win, I couldn't suffer defeat again so near the end, could I? When I learned that the game had ended 1-0 to Manchester United (from my compatriot Nani's goal), I felt sure that I had won. I watched the highlights on Sky News. I was still calm, but I saw I had been very lucky that a greater number of shots hadn't found the back of the Manchester United net, with Berbatov and Robbie Keane getting very close to scoring. I was even more confident of my victory now luck was on my side. I asked myself, have I finally worked hard enough to deserve it? The table was updated and there was my name in first place! The winning feeling started to creep in and it was amazing; this time I could really do it. There was still one more game to go between Middlesbrough and Newcastle, but there were no major threats among the players in those teams. It finished 2-2, with no player standing out, so I didn't expect it to have much effect on the final result, but I had to wait for the final confirmation. The following Monday was a Bank Holiday in England, so the wait lasted until Tuesday. I went to work as normal, controlling my anxiety levels as much as I could.

When I finally saw the up-to-date table, I was the winner. My winning team was called 'The Best of Me 2', a name that I chose based on the lyrics from a song of the same name from the English band The Darkness. I sent a short message to my girlfriend telling her that I'd won, and I remember writing something related to the lyrics of that song – I did what I did for you ... you've got the best of me! Patricia told me that it confirmed what she thought – that I could go very far and that I was capable of achieving something special. I felt proud and a bit relieved as she had contributed some money to 'our' investment and it had paid off so quickly! We were a team. And we were winning together! I got the official email and I was asked to send some photos and answer some questions for the competition's official blog. I held a football that said 'Winner' on it and asked my mum to take me some pictures in the Palace of Queluz area near where I lived. I was wearing a suit and tie in a classic but formal style. I think I did it because I remember that the photo of the winner of the 2006 World Cup fantasy football competition was wearing a suit, when I had been so close to being in the photo myself. Now it was my moment, and my picture would be printed in the *Daily Mirror* the next day. I had struggled so much to reach this level and my wish had finally been fulfilled. The £10,000 prize was a great help financially and I was able to finally forget the pain from my previous defeats. I had been able to perform at my best and reach the number-one spot. The 'You The Manager' staff announced my win on the homepage, stating that, 'Rui hopes this victory will bring him one step closer to working alongside his idol, fellow Portuguese national José Mourinho'. The *Daily Mirror* put my picture on the 'You The Manager' page with a nice headline: 'Big Rui makes Marq'. Now it was more than just a dream, it was reality.

7

KEEPING THE
LEVEL HIGH

I decided after my big win that I wouldn't tell many
people. I didn't tell any of my co-workers or many
members of my family. I thought that some people could
get jealous, and if they knew I had won a substantial
amount of money they might not be very kind. I am the
sort of person who doesn't need to show off, I prefer to
appear quiet and more introverted than the other way
around. I also wanted to continue on the path of victory,
and I wanted to make sure I had as few distractions to
put me off track as possible.

I did not want to be a sort of 'one-hit wonder', an
expression that defines someone who conquers something
and has huge success for a short period of time then
disappears. And I knew I had the quality to be consistent
and keep winning. I just needed to stay focussed, continue
with my work and I was sure more victories would come. I
wanted to fight for more wins as 'Manager of the Month',
but also had eyes on 'Manager of the Year'. Incredibly, and
ironically, the day I went to the bank to deposit the cheque
for my August victory, news came out that José Mourinho
had been sacked from Chelsea! What a coincidence!

I remained solid in the overall rankings as the season continued, chasing first place. I remember a game in which Martin Laursen, a Danish defender from Aston Villa, surprisingly scored two goals, which helped me a lot as he was one of my big season picks as a complementary defender to the blocks from the top teams. However, I didn't do so well in the September monthly competition, and in October I only managed to finish in the top 20. But in November things started to change.

I prepared very well for the monthly competition in November, separating out the teams that were no longer in the running for the season competition and recycling them by making some substitutions after studying the fixtures for the month. It is very important to understand which teams have the easiest set of matches each month and, even more crucially, to know which teams will play more games. You can't predict a result, but you can find out if a team will play one or two more matches than another, and that can be crucial.

I had performed consistently all month, and with only one match to go I was in second place, but with a considerable points difference between me and the leading team, managed by 'The Syndicate' and called '241'. I guess this was probably a group of people who played together and had a lot of teams! The last match was between Blackburn Rovers and Aston Villa, and, although I didn't know which players my opponent had, I felt the player in my team that could make a difference was John Carew, a big Norwegian striker from Aston Villa. In the past, I had already lost twice in the last game when I was leading, so why couldn't I do the opposite and steal the lead on the last match? I had no real reason for my optimism, but I was determined to fight to the end and keep hopeful. I started to follow the game, obviously supporting Aston Villa and hoping for a good performance from Carew, and in the 29th minute the Norwegian scored! By my calculations, a goal and an assist from Carew would be enough to help me grab first place, so everything was to play for. Aston Villa were the best team on the night, and in the end they trashed Blackburn 4-0 and, after some more good luck, I knew I would get more points because of an assist by Carew later in the second half. A feeling of nerves and anxiety took over! I thought I could be on my way to a second win in the monthly competition. I was right, I managed to win, and incredibly I also had another team in second place, which also had Carew in it, as well as Ashley Young, the gifted Aston Villa winger, who had also scored! My prize money was £10,000 for first place, plus £1,000 for second – fantastic! What a sensational performance: in just four months of the competition I already had two wins as 'Manager of the Month'! The next day my name and the news about my win were mentioned in the *Daily Mirror* newspaper again.

By the beginning of December, I was leading the overall table, but I started to make some mistakes and had a terrible month. Influenced by the Aston Villa team performance that had been instrumental in my November win, I started to bet a lot on this team, particularly on their defenders. In my team with the best chance in the overall leader board, I made one desperate, all-or-nothing move in January, building a defence almost completely from Aston Villa's players, with Scott Carson as goalkeeper and Martin Laursen, Zat Knight (who had started the season at Fulham so didn't count as an Aston Villa player) and Wilfred Bouma as defenders. From the usual Villa defensive quartet, only

Olaf Mellberg was not in my team, and the other defender I had was George McCartney from West Ham. The rest of my team was strong, with good midfielders and forwards, because I had the budget for it as I didn't spend too much on the defenders. Every weekend I hoped that Aston Villa would not concede any goals as that would determine whether or not I went up in the table. The team coach I had chosen was Martin O'Neill, whom I greatly admired and gave me confidence. In the recent past he had been getting results wherever he went, namely with Leicester and Celtic. As a player, he had also been trained by the legendary Brian Clough, in his prime, at Nottingham Forest.

I knew the strategy was risky, but I was clear on the reasons I had chosen this team: from my analysis, I felt Aston Villa's defensive players had been undervalued – which left me with a good budget to sign a reasonable number of top players for my midfield and attack positions, while still having a strong defence. I thought there was a high probability that no goals would be conceded in a number of Aston Villa's games in the last half of the season, which further justified my move. What I didn't see coming was Aston Villa's poor run of conceding goals in 15 games in a row! That killed my strategy. Every weekend that Aston Villa were playing, I hoped that my position in the table would improve, but in the end the result was always the same. My frustration reached a peak after two weeks in February/March. In the first week Aston Villa were beating Reading 2-0 and they had the game won, but in the last kick of the game, a free kick, Nicky Shorey scored a goal for Reading, which blew another clean sheet. I remember a friend of mine, who knew about my strategy and was watching the game, told me that he was getting ready to call me to congratulate me and say that my recovery was underway when that goal came! But I was so strong now that I managed to overcome my disappointment and I remember saying to him the next week, in the away game against Arsenal, that I would recover the points! I watched the game from start to finish, but it was another tough blow because Aston Villa were winning 1-0 until they conceded an equaliser from Bendtner in injury time, the game ending 1-1. In two consecutive weeks I lost the 'clean sheet' after the 90th minute! It was hard to bear. I remember receiving another blow when they were at home to Sunderland and they conceded in the 83rd minute for a 1-0 surprise home defeat. I was not playing well in the monthly competition, and my challenge for the overall title was fading away fast.

In the final stretch of the championship, there was a glimmer of hope when Aston Villa didn't concede a goal in two consecutive matches and the rest of my team also performed well. I was back in the game, reaching the top ten! This proved that my strategy was not as bad as it had been starting to look, but I had simply been unlucky. With two matches to go for Villa, the next one being at home to Wigan, I had a slight hope of a top-five finish – maybe. But after that game my hopes disintegrated after a 2-0 loss. I didn't even finish in the top 30 after another inconsistent performance from them in the last match of the season against West Ham, resulting in a 2-2 draw, and they missed out on the Europa League as well.

The season was over, but I still had a lot to be positive about as I won two 'Manager of the Month' awards for the first time. I won two big prizes, so I wasn't the guy who always falls at the last hurdle anymore. I was the star of the competition for the first half of the season, and I was honoured to be interviewed for the competition's blog. To be more successful in the future, I needed to improve my early scores even more to be in with a chance of winning 'Manager of the Year', which would also avoid the need for me to apply all-or-nothing strategies, like I had last season. The winner that year was a Croatian who had made a considerable investment and had almost double the number of teams I had, but he was a good competitor and a deserving winner. I think I had some bad luck and deserved a top-ten finish at least, but I could learn from it and hopefully be better next year. As with everything in my life, I had to be patient, persistent and get up again.

8

MARRIAGE AND VICTORY ... WELL ALMOST

Saturday, 30 August 2008

No, this was not the day the English league started, but it was the day I got married and started a new chapter in my life. It had been a long courtship (more than nine years) and marriage was the next natural step in a relationship that had been so important to my success, and I hoped it would give me the stability I needed to win again in the future. We were happy that we would finally be living together and waking up side-by-side every day. We didn't want a traditional Portuguese party with hundreds of guests, as we didn't feel that we had enough money to justify it. We didn't have a honeymoon, or a traditional bridal gown for Patricia either, but she still looked beautiful in her dress. I wore a new suit that my mother had given me for the occasion. At the last minute, after some pressure from close family, we booked a lunch at an expensive restaurant, but only for a very small group of people. We couldn't splash money as we desperately wanted to save money to buy furniture for our new home – a three-bedroom flat with a fantastic attic and a bright living room with a nice view of the sea. My fantasy football skills were the best way for us to move closer to achieving a better life at the time, despite both of us having good prospects in terms of our current jobs in finance. Patricia and I felt the same way and we knew what our priorities should be. Maybe because of the wedding, I didn't start the championship as strong as I had the previous season. I didn't repeat my win in the August monthly competition, but my number-one goal of the season was to win the annual prize of £100,000.

There was a very popular forum on the internet at the time called FISO, which was a good platform for conversation between competitors. I liked to write posts and I always followed what was going on there. When I was on there once, I saw a thread about betting odds for the future winner of 'You The Manager' in 2008/09. The Croatian, the current champion, was considered the out-and-out favourite, but the second person with slightly lower odds to win was me! This gave me great confidence and I thought they must see me as a fierce competitor, even though I hadn't even finished in the top 20 in the annual competition. From the forum, I was also flattered by an invitation from the 2005/06 winner, and now a good friend, Darren Ingram, who wanted me to join his 'mini-league' – and I accepted. (I have mentioned how these work in a previous chapter.) There were some good prizes in this parallel competition, and the leaders of each one were trying to get the best players to enter.

I had an excellent run in October and came close to winning the monthly prize, but victory narrowly escaped me as I finished in second, third and fourth with three separate teams. It was frustrating. I never found out which players were in the monthly winner's team, so all I could do was hope that I was performing well and that luck just hadn't been on my side. I had to move on. Nowadays, I don't regret these defeats, because if they hadn't happened I wouldn't have had the strength and the experiences that led me to win what I've won, and my victories have appeased all of my most frustrating defeats. Anyway, the cash prizes I won for the places on the podium that month had already paid for my investment that season, so I was under no pressure at all in financial terms.

I was fully dedicated and focussed in the following months, and I reached first place in the overall table by around December, curiously at the same time that I went to spend a weekend in the north to buy furniture for my almost empty flat. The kitchen was fully equipped but when we got married the only other thing we had was an old, small wooden table that had the TV on it. I used to use it to put my laptop on when I was working on my teams. Our big purchase of the first months was a decent sofa so we could sit and watch TV more comfortably. We lived in the attic mainly, and we were still sleeping on Patricia's single bed, which was OK but we couldn't do it forever. By February/ March time, the last third of the season, I was still leading the overall table. Players like Michael Turner, the English defender from Hull City who could be called an 'enabler' (a low budget defender who would allow more money to be spent on other players), or Tim Cahill, an Australian attacking midfielder from Everton, who came back from an injury but whom I had a good feeling about, were all proving to be good shouts. In a derby game between Liverpool and Everton, Cahill scored the equaliser in injury time and I remember celebrating as if I had scored the goal, sliding on my knees!

After a midweek set of fixtures in February, a gap of 28 points opened up between me and second place, which was very good. I started to feel that the title was almost mine, and I had everything I needed to keep hold of the advantage, including two substitutions. But I started to crumble a bit because two of my forwards, Anelka and Berbatov, had a bit of a dry period. I faced some additional unexpected problems: Anelka was playing out of position – now a winger – and Berbatov was benched in a few games – no longer the first choice for Alex Ferguson. Even so, I was still leading overall on 9 April, 15 points above the second-placed team and more than 30 points above third place. But the pressure increased for me after a fantastic match in which eight goals were scored: the final result was Liverpool 4 Arsenal 4. Arsenal's Russian player, Arshavin, scored four goals, which meant a total of 28 points! One of the top-five competitors jumped up the table and was now really close to catching me.

Sunday, 26 April 2009

With five weeks to go, I was not strong enough to handle the pressure of seeing my advantage slip away. I was now in second place, nine points behind the leader, and I made the mistake that would cost me the victory. I used the two substitutions I had left to bring in Fernando Torres and John Carew for Anelka and Berbatov. Immediately, in one of the first games of the weekend, my Everton defender Phil Jagielka injured himself after a solo run, damaging his knee ligaments. I felt like I had lost everything. I was going to be playing with ten men until the end of the season! Plus, some of my rivals had Everton defenders and they were still in the FA Cup, which also counted for scoring. I tried to stay calm and keep my cool. I had made these substitutions because the players I introduced were in good shape and had a much easier set of fixtures in the run up to the end of the season – the plan could still work.

But the following weekend I completely lost my cool and realised that I was going to lose. Anelka returned to scoring goals. My opponents who had not had any substitutions left (or had only one) had been forced to keep him, but this limitation had proved to be beneficial in the end. The French striker that I had replaced started to crush me, scoring and assisting against Fulham. I hoped that Fernando Torres would score a miraculous hat-trick against Newcastle the next day and that would be my answer.

To avoid stressing too much, I went to the Estoril Open tournament on Sunday, the most prestigious tennis event in Portugal. I took a look at a TV that was broadcasting the game while I was there and I realised that the Spanish striker wasn't even on the bench. I couldn't handle it and I threw my mobile phone on the floor – fortunately it was grass, and I didn't break it! It was too much for me, this series of events was holding me back. And the slow descent down the table continued until the end of the season, when I finally stopped in tenth place – but at least I finished in the top ten, which was my highest finish so far. The winner turned out to be an English competitor – he had had Arshavin and luck on his side when I had made my fatal mistake. Again, I had not been clever enough, I had to think through my mistakes and come back stronger next season.

To make things a little bit better, I won a consolation prize from my friend Darren Ingram's mini-league. We won the annual mini-league championship and I contributed to the win with five teams! Despite my heavy fall in the last month of the competition, I still managed to finish with five teams in the top 100. It was agreed to give £600 to each team that had contributed to the win, so Darren sent me a cheque for £3,000! As I was in my first year of marriage and still furnishing the house, it came in very handy! Darren was very kind to me that season – after my tough defeat he sent me the poem 'If' by Rudyard Kipling, one of the lines in which reads: 'If you can meet with Triumph and Disaster and treat those two impostors just the same way' and ends with the conclusion at the end of the poem '... you'll be a Man'. I saw this poem as the perfect incentive for me to find balance again – the underlying message is that in life you need to be prepared for the good and bad moments, and you will only be a man when you can cope with them both and keep your balance.

The defeat made me think of my idol Nigel Mansell and how he had lost the 1986 Formula One Championship near the end of the last race in Australia, when one of the car's tyres had blown. My path had similarities to his. Out of frustration and anger, I published a post on the FISO forum titled 'How I Lost £100,000.' I regret it and was heavily criticised by the other contenders – and they were right. I wrote that 'a guy who deserves to win this less than me will win', which I must say wasn't true. But I also expressed that I would keep on working hard and try to be champion next season, which was most definitely the truth.

After the season was over I was depressed for some time, and I only came through near the beginning of the new season. The best way for me to overcome it was by listening to music and lyrics that resonated with me and helped me to feel better and look forward to the future with optimism. Music is very important to me when I am down, but I don't know how to play a single instrument. I admire and enjoy listening to amazing sharpened voices like Freddie Mercury, Karen Carpenter or Elis Regina. My favourite band is Queen but I also love Manic Street Preachers and The Darkness.

9

MORE THAN PERFECT

The new season was about to begin. The prize for the overall winner this year was now only £75,000, which was disappointing after the £100,000-win had narrowly escaped me last year. But I thought to myself, 'If I can get £75,000 I would still be very happy, so let's move on!' The monthly prizes were also cut in half – £5,000 instead of £10,000.

I started my preparation, and my level of motivation reached a new high! Like every year, I took a few days off before the start of the season, and I shut myself away at home from morning to night so I could concentrate solely on my teams, preparing them to be the best they possibly could. The biggest change in the transfer market had been the exit of Cristiano Ronaldo to Real Madrid. It would make the final decisions more interesting as one of the mandatory players had left, which meant more uncertainty. It was another variable that had to be thought through and it would create more differences between the teams. The rules had also changed: there were now no limits on the number of players that could be selected from the same team.

It was probably the best preparation I had ever made, and I made a strong start. In my usual start-up strategy, I built a few teams with a defensive block from a lower-rated club, this season using Stoke City. You had to play a 4-3-3, so amongst the goalkeeper and three Stoke defenders, I added Liverpool defender Glen Johnson, as I wasn't sure who would play in one of the defensive positions for Stoke and it was better not to risk it. As there were only a small number of matches to play before the end of the month, I thought I was well placed to win the August monthly competition again, just like two years before – second only to a competitor from Hungary. He was probably the biggest investor of all, and it was annoying to see how many teams had been registered on his behalf. I think that everybody should invest freely, but this seemed over the top and unfair to me. I think he had at least three times as many teams as me.

I tried to figure out who were the 11 players in his team, as there were no substitutions allowed in the first month. I made my calculations by analysing the changes in his points, and I came to the annoying conclusion that our teams were almost the same, with only one different player – he had Luka Modric from Tottenham and I had Niko Kranjcar from Portsmouth, by coincidence both of whom were Croatians. The problem was, in addition to having more points than me, his player Modric played at home against Birmingham, which was theoretically easier than Kranjcar's game, which was also at home but was against Newcastle. Modric played in his match on the Saturday and I followed the game, obviously wanting him to score as few points as possible. He only scored two points after leaving the game because of an injury. That being the case, I needed Kranjcar to score a goal to give me six bonus points, and a total of eight points would put me in first place. When it was time for the game on Sunday, I followed it from start to finish, but it was a very average match. I didn't even get excited at the possibility of a goal, it was such a loose display from Portsmouth and Kranjcar. In all honesty, he wasn't my favourite player as he didn't seem to want to play, and he wasn't aggressive enough in my opinion, despite having good technical skills. Modric was a better player, but he was not effective for Tottenham, scoring an average of three goals per season, and he was still adapting to the English league. So, I went for Kranjcar over Modric, but this decision went against me. I finished August in second place and the Hungarian won. I won a few pounds with that podium finish, but again I was beginning to get labelled as an almost winner and I hated it. After my two great victories in August and November 2007, I was missing winning. The game took place on my first wedding anniversary and I remember taking a picture of me and Patricia to mark the date, but my unhappiness at not celebrating it with a victory was written all over my face.

So, I recovered from the defeat very quickly, and it was on to September, and my 30th birthday! My previous second-place finish meant that I would start the attack in a good position. I had some other teams that had started well and were well placed too. I made a few changes to the teams when the season substitutions were allowed, and I easily reached first place overall. I was also going strong in the September monthly competition and I started the last weekend with some of my teams in the top ten. I had some substitutions left to make in the teams I had built for the monthly prizes and my strategy was to change the defensive block of each one, hoping that one of those blocks wouldn't concede any goals. Again, the block from Manchester United, with the bonus of John O'Shea scoring a goal, led me to believe that I could be in first place. That Saturday I was in Beja, a town in the south of Portugal, at my company's Family Day – an initiative where the workers' families met for team-building activities and were able to socialise. I remember trying some sports for the first time in my life, like rowing and archery. Patricia also enjoyed some new experiences. The food at the event was excellent, and we tasted some new flavours that were specialties of the region. It was a welcome distraction, but I couldn't completely switch off, stopping every now and then to think about the Premier League football matches that were happening all over the weekend.

When the tables were updated, to my disappointment I found my team in second place and Eoghan, an Irishman who had already beaten me in the final match of a monthly competition and in the 2006 World Cup, was in the lead! I just remember thinking, 'Not again! Am I cursed?' The reason he was now leading was (in addition to the Manchester United block) Tottenham's Robbie Keane, who had scored four goals on Saturday. But I still had two Sunderland players playing on Sunday against Hull City. I needed goals from my cheapest midfielder, Andy Reid, and Darren Bent, the excellent Sunderland striker. Mathematically, I needed at least one goal and an assist. This time I had to overcome Eoghan, who likely didn't have any players left to play – I couldn't finish in second place again! I watched the game, and it didn't start badly as Darren Bent scored his first goal right at the beginning! I was closer now. Following a corner, Andy Reid crossed and Michael Turner, one of my players from the cruel defeat in the 2008/09 season, scored! I got bonus points for Reid's assist, which should have put me in first place. To squash any doubts, Bent scored another and the game ended 5-2. I was sure I'd won the September monthly! I couldn't sleep I was so anxious from Sunday to Monday and went to work waiting for the final results. My victory was confirmed, it was my return to the top places and my third win in the monthly prizes, the same month that I turned 30! A milestone in my life, my career, and I had beaten my most annoying rival.

Two weeks later I received a request from the 'You The Manager' team for an interview, to be published on the YouTube channel for the contest. It went well, and it is still online today, and it is always good to be linked with this kind of initiative. The reason for the interview was not only the monthly win, but also the overall leadership, which was still my main goal at the time.

The season went on and I stayed in front. I survived the difficult Christmas and New Year period without any problems, knowing already from previous experience that this is crucial because many games are played in a short period of time. However, I never managed to get a good lead. I was up and down, but always in the top five. I had some moments of weakness; in January, for example, Clint Dempsey (a good cheap midfielder from Fulham) picked up a serious injury and I was forced to replace him. Seeing me sad and moaning, my wife asked me, 'so, are you not as good as you think?' It was everything I didn't want to hear, but at the same time it was all I needed to hear. I had to set up my teams again and regain my composure. I had another tough moment when Liverpool hosted Portsmouth, and I was hoping that my goalkeeper, Reina, and my Liverpool defenders, Agger and Arbeloa, would not concede, but within minutes of the end Belhadj scored for Portsmouth.

I don't cry easily, but the tears welled in my eyes after such a big loss of points with that late goal. I had some moments of fragility; for example, I chose Drogba over Rooney and when the Englishman scored a brace in a match I felt that I could go down again. But my team was excellent: when one player failed, another would appear and score, as happened in a game in which Darren Bent voided Rooney's good performance from the day before. Signs were starting to show that this time I could have the winning team.

One day, in the middle of the night, I woke up thinking about my team – it was not a rare situation to be honest – and decided to swap Liverpool defender Arbeloa for Tottenham's Gareth Bale. I had seen some of Bale's recent games and he was already in his third season at Spurs but had not yet shown his full potential. Using the same intuition I had with Schweinsteiger back in 2006, I thought Bale was close to 'exploding' and showing his enormous quality. On top of this, he counted as a defender and was playing as a left-winger, which is always something a good fantasy football player should spot. And his price was very low, £3 million, so I decided to sign him. Then, in a midweek match, Gareth Bale scored against Arsenal, which would mean a massive bonus of eight points because a defender had scored a goal! I went running in to tell my wife! At that moment, I felt that luck was on my side again. The following weekend, Bale scored again and it was an excellent goal against Chelsea! He was becoming a key player for me and only one of my rivals had also picked him. The rest of the team were also playing well. I had to take out Arsenal player Cesc Fabregas after a serious injury, but I made a good choice for his replacement, opting for Chelsea winger Florent Malouda. The other two midfielders I had were Frank Lampard and

Steven Gerrard – it was a strong midfield that, strategically, I decided to build and hold. Another player that was a good bet was the much-criticised Nicklas Bendtner of Arsenal, who was scoring goals regularly and was relatively cheap to buy. With four weeks remaining till the end of the season, my team was Reina, Agger, Ivanovic, Bale, Baines, Lampard, Malouda, Gerrard, Drogba, Bent and Bendtner. And I still had a substitution left. I was not going to make the same stupid mistake as last year and run out of replacements too soon.

Sunday, 25 April 2010

This was the day of a key game: Burnley versus Liverpool. My direct rivals for the win didn't have Steven Gerrard, and I knew that a good performance from him could be a deciding factor. The final result was Burnley 0 Liverpool 4, with two goals from Gerrard. One of my opponents wrote something very pertinent in the FISO forum: 'after a marathon, we were entering the stadium already tired and Rui appears and starts to sprint'. I was in first place, more than 15 points ahead, for the first time that season. Soon after were the penultimate round of games, and a big match: Liverpool versus Chelsea. I decided to make my last substitution, which turned out to be a wise decision. Even knowing Liverpool were playing at home, I took out Daniel Agger and I put in John Terry. I needed to be careful because I knew that my opponents who could catch me up had more Chelsea defenders than me and I needed to counteract this. The final result was Liverpool 0 Chelsea 2. I thought I'd made a brilliant move and had learned my lesson from the previous year very well! One of the Chelsea goals was scored by Drogba after a bad back pass from Gerrard, and as a joke someone wrote in the forum, 'is Rui going to claim Gerrard's assist?' They had been in a good mood because they thought I'd lost ground after Chelsea's clean sheet, but they didn't realise that I'd taken out a defender who lost the game and put in a defender who won it. After that I think everyone realised I had everything under control.

As the last round came, my greatest fear was a good score for Chelsea's Nicolas Anelka, who my immediate rival had in their team. I was afraid of being crushed by the Frenchman, as I had been in the previous season, and Chelsea had a title match waiting, in which they had the potential to score heavily against Wigan, with Anelka in good shape! The final score was 8-0 for the new English champions! Anelka played his part with two goals, but at the same time my saviour Gareth Bale also scored for Tottenham and everything stayed equal in the table. Only the FA Cup Final was left and my dream was close to becoming a reality. The game was between Chelsea and Portsmouth at Wembley. The only thing that could make me lose my cool was if something odd should happen, like a match with lots of goals or more than one goal from a defender.

I spent the week feeling tremendously anxious, but went to work as usual and counted down the days until the big match. I remember dealing with what I felt was an unfair situation at work on one of those days, and I had to listen to a colleague shout at me as she pointed out something that she thought I'd done wrong. But I looked at her and just thought to myself I'm on my way to winning £75,000, you can scream as loud as you like but I'm not bothered. Reflecting on it now, I remember that after joining the company back in December 2006, I spent more than three years as a temporary employee, and I was often treated differently by the company. But I knew that the stability this job gave me was crucial to my success in fantasy football, my parallel career and my escape. Nobody at my workplace knew that I was chasing a big win or that I had had so much success over the previous years.

Sunday, 15 May 2010

The FA Cup Final – I decided not to watch the game. During the game time I watched a DVD of my favourite 80s TV series instead – *Family Ties*, starring Michael J. Fox, one of my all-time favourite actors. I had time to see maybe five or six episodes, but after more than an hour of watching it I was already fed up and my nerves were getting the better of me, so I went to take a shower. When I finished, I looked at the clock and realised that the game would probably be over. It was possible that the game had gone into extra time, but I didn't think that was likely as Chelsea were massive favourites. I had decided to stay at home – maybe a good thing, maybe not, but I thought it was the best place to be – and I remember I put my laptop on my desk in the attic where I have always felt a very positive energy, so I wanted to know my fate there. I walked upstairs and went to check the result on the internet: Chelsea 1 Portsmouth 0 and a Didier Drogba goal! I thought surely I was the winner of 'You The Manager' 2009/10! It was the final step after years and years of sacrifice and commitment, but it was all worthwhile. The feeling of winning the season-long contest played by hundreds of thousands of people from many countries around the world was unbelievable. I felt on top of the world. All the disappointment I'd felt from those difficult defeats over the years was well and truly gone. I don't remember showing any emotions; I just felt everything inside. I didn't need to party, I already felt amazingly well, and I knew that my wife felt the same. She is like me, but even more calm and introvert. She doesn't need to scream or smile to express her emotions. She was genuinely happy, but we both kept our composure. We probably seem a bit boring, but that's the way we are. I knew she was feeling the same as me. We did it together. I remember making some phone calls, but nothing particularly important, and then it was time to enjoy the moment. The name of my team was 'Affection 13' – I had decided to give each team the name of an emotion, and I won with the name of a very beautiful one, which could be interpreted as something symbolic!

I knew that the *Daily Mirror* newspaper were going to report my win at some point during the next week, and I went to do a photoshoot at the national stadium for the article. I wore a suit with a red-and-black tie that I had purposely bought over a year before to wear if I ever managed to win. It was positive wishful thinking, but it really happened. The 'You The Manager' team asked me for a photo with a glass of champagne, but in the end they published a photo of me in my living room. The interview and the story filled a page of the newspaper. It was everything I had dreamed of. There was also a reference to José Mourinho in the title of the interview: 'Marques is Mour' (pun with 'Mour'inho) than delighted'. And I still had the icing on the cake to come: at the end of the season the perfect team of the season was published, with the best players by sector and the respective points, and my team's score had beaten that perfect 11! It was the first time that had happened. The reason for this is that the substitutions I made were accurate and at the right time, which made me able to catch the best periods for several players. It was tough to win a championship, but I did it in glorious style, breaking records – just like Nigel Mansell in 1992 when he won the Formula One title with nine wins out of 16.

The win meant we could finally buy some quality things for our living room and fill the space with a big TV, a big table, a nice sofa and some chairs. Although, even today, I still go crazy when I remember that Patricia spent a bit too much on two red chairs that were well designed and beautiful, but were really quite expensive.

The 2010 World Cup competition was still to come, and I was asked to advertise it. The *Daily Mirror* had the idea of using a photo of me with the following sentence below: 'the great thing about YTM is that you need a level of skill to win, it's not just pot luck'. I was honoured, but in the competition itself I didn't perform well. Spain were the champions, but I bet on Argentina. It had already been the best season of my life, and I had no energy for more. I deserved a rest now and needed time to prepare to defend my title in 2010/11.

10

DECENT BUT NOT GOOD ENOUGH

I started the 2010/11 season with a major new goal – defend my title – it was a new feeling and it increased the pressure I felt. I felt motivated though, and I knew that I had to be at my best, but today, looking back, I think I lacked a bit of the fire and appetite I'd had the previous year. My obsession with being champion had been rewarded, and now I was a little bit more relaxed. The first big decision of the season happened in the fight for the September monthly prize, and I arrived at the last day of the month with three teams well positioned to clinch the win. Incredibly, I played well. I'd distributed the defensive blocks from the stronger league teams at the time, but the only teams that didn't concede goals that weekend were teams from the bottom of the table. My Hungarian rival won again, apparently betting on a block from a less-revered team. However, I had one player in my best team for the overall competition, Arsenal's Samir Nasri, who had excelled that week, but I'd excluded him from my best teams for the monthly competition. So, despite the defeat, I had a team for the overall competition that was very strong and was in the top five for many months. It had fulfilled my first goal, to be in the fight for the title again. In November I was again well positioned to fight for the win in the monthly competition. I was in second place with one set of fixtures left to play. I managed to pass the leader, but I was overtaken by the third-place team, who went on to win that month. After four months, in the monthly competitions I had already had a third and a second-place finish, and I was earning decent money and regular prizes in the mini-leagues competition. Almost every month, I took home cheques, although I was starting to get frustrated with the flurry of podium finishes that were never the top place.

By the time we reached March, I found myself in a strange position in the overall leader boards: I was in second place, some way ahead of third place but more than 30 points behind the guy in first place – a competitor who had been in the top ten in the previous season but not a guy who was used to winning. Nevertheless, he was performing really well and took a big lead. After that followed weeks and weeks of trauma, and I couldn't get close to him. I remember he had Bolton's Kevin Davies, a striker I would never choose because I thought he was limited technically, but he was scoring and assisting consistently, even in the FA Cup. I remember commenting to my wife that I was having a great season and I could chase the leader, but his team was perfect, everything he touched turned to gold. There were moments when I thought, 'I need to keep calm, I'm sure he'll slip, I know that it is not easy to lead, and I'm sure he'll suffer from the pressure. So, I can't lose my cool and take big risks.' I remember my eternal favourite Lampard scoring two goals in a game and helping me recover a bit, but I was not closing enough of the gap. In April, with the end of the championship approaching, I had to react and needed something magic to happen, so I had to pull a rabbit from the hat – I went to Dirk Kuyt from Liverpool. It was a bit of a risky move, but he helped me recover slightly. But with three games to go, I made a silly mistake again – instead of using my last substitution for a Manchester City defender who would be in the FA Cup Final against Stoke, I bought Manchester United defender Evra, who was already thinking more about the Champions League Final. My second option had been to buy Joleon Lescott from Manchester City, but my final decision had been the wrong one. My reason was that although Manchester City were in the cup final and that meant an extra game, they were going to neglect the championship and concede goals, so it wouldn't pay off to take the easy and most logical route. I tried to be different and I failed. The Manchester City defence didn't concede any goals in the cup final, played before the end of the championship (which was very rare), nor in the last games of the championship. The teams with the Manchester City defence emerged and ascended up the rankings, and the leader himself, who had led the table for so long, was equalled and had to share his first place with another competitor in the end, who also had a lot of Manchester City defenders. I ended up in a modest sixth place, but my second team, which had the Manchester City defence, moved up to seventh place. I finished with two teams in the top ten and that gave me some money. Today I regret not being more conservative because that would have guaranteed me a top-three finish, but for me, playing as the defending champion, I only wanted to play one way: first or nothing. It was hard to think any other way. Anyway, there were no excuses, I had failed and didn't deserve to win. But for the fourth consecutive season I managed to finish in the top ten, which is an achievement that only those who understand this kind of competition will know how hard it is.

That summer, Chelsea hired André Villas-Boas, a new Portuguese coach who had won everything at FC Porto the previous season, including the Europa League. So, I had an idea, which I now think was ridiculous, although it was still a learning experience for me. In July 2011 I decided to build a portfolio of all the reports of my fantasy football success from the newspapers plus the print-outs of my winning teams. I went to London to try and deliver it to the new Chelsea coach. I told my wife what I planned to do and she agreed I should give it a try. Even if I failed, at least we would get to visit London and see the sights, which would justify the money it would cost. I went to the training centre in Cobham, which was a long walk (my wife was with me), but the security guard wouldn't let me go through. Then I did a tour at the stadium and club museum, and the tour guide told me to leave my portfolio in the reception and it would be delivered to André. I did just that, and I also tried to talk to other members of the Chelsea staff, but without success. I came back to Lisbon with a mission partly accomplished. At least we got to visit Wimbledon while we were there, though. We also went to the street where Freddie Mercury lived in South Kensington, which was very emotional for both of us. Later, I made an even more absurd attempt when I went to Coimbra (a city in the centre of Portugal) to deliver another copy of my portfolio to the President of Villas-Boas's former club, Académica de Coimbra – he was a good friend of his and had been the first person to give André a chance as coach two years before. I never got any feedback, and months later Villas-Boas was fired from Chelsea.

My first attempt to enter the real football industry was a total fiasco, so I had to shift my mind back to fantasy football and prepare for the 2011/12 season. This season, the company that usually ran 'You The Manager' had been replaced, and the rules were changed substantially. The prize money had dropped too. To be fair, the new company made a huge effort to manage the competition the best way they could, but unfortunately they failed. Some of the players' prices didn't make any sense, in particular the top players, who were far too expensive. I think they realised their error, but in trying to compensate for it they made another one: the players who were signed after the launch of the competition were given a much lower price. The worst example I can remember was Sergio Aguero, who was bought by Manchester City days before the league started and had a pathetically low price. I know that one of the secrets to success in fantasy football is spotting this type of undervaluation, but something so obvious became embarrassing and reduced the prestige of the contest. Another new rule was the option to choose from several formations instead of the traditional rigid 4-3-3.

This season turned out to be my worst ever; I wasn't able to adapt, and I didn't develop any understanding of the new competition rules. It was a difficult period for me personally too. My wife broke her arm in November 2011 – she was running to catch a train after work and she fell on the train station floor! It was her second fall in just a few days, after she had started wearing a new pair of boots she'd bought from America on the internet. She had to have surgery, but it went wrong. Her body reacted badly to the anaesthetic and she was in intensive care for a day, but it felt more like a week. It was a terrible experience for us. I was distraught. In February 2012 she had further surgery to remove pins from her arm that were already digging into her skin. Patricia is vital to my stability and performance, and without her I just wasn't the same person. Fortunately, she has now fully recovered.

As the season came to a close, I had one last fight left in me, going after the monthly prize for April. On the last day I needed Manchester United to keep a clean sheet against Everton, but the game finished 4-4 and destroyed my last hope of glory in this disastrous season. One situation that I remember in particular really epitomised my poor performance: I had bought Newcastle striker Demba Ba as he was having a good season, but soon after I made my move it was the other striker from Newcastle, the recent signing Papiss Cisse, who started scoring in almost every game, while Demba Ba went through a dry patch. It seemed like everything I touched was cursed. For the first time since 2007 I reached the end of the season completely out of the title fight, finishing in 14th place, which I still rate as honourable given the number of complications I'd had along the way.

The best decision I made that season was to enter three teams in a contest organised by the German newspaper *Bild* but produced by the English company that used to run 'You The Manager'. The previous season, I had entered three teams and was in the process of studying and understanding the German league. My results that season suggested that I could have a future in the game, as I finished in the top 200, even without a full focus and speaking hardly any German. There were a large number of participants, around 200,000, and to win it would be a great new challenge for me. Everything about this new game was great, and

I remember telling my wife that I thought the rules and the points system were impressive, almost perfect. I also told my father that there was another interesting German fantasy football competition, and he told me that maybe we'd be celebrating a victory in Germany one day. At the time I didn't care that much because my priority was to repeat my win in England. But I didn't forget what he said, and it made more sense, quite unexpectedly, not long after.

11

FAIRY TALE IN GERMANY

By July 2012 all my personal problems from the previous season were behind me. I was determined to change my focus, and I decided on a new goal – to fight for the title in the German *BILD* 'Super Manager', which had a prize of €100,000 for the overall winner. The English newspapers started excluding players who were not residents in the United Kingdom, which made the decision even more straightforward.

It was the first time I'd had a proper attempt at the German competition, and I studied hard so I could give it my best shot and hopefully achieve results as soon as possible. I studied the German language – a friend lent me dictionaries and introduction books and I dedicated my free time to learning it. Another of my pre-season goals was to buy and study two magazines: an annual Portuguese publication and a German one published by the newspaper *Kicker*, which were guides to the Bundesliga season. After being unable to get hold of them, I booked a day's holiday in August to travel to Cascais (a very touristy city in Portugal) to search for them. I couldn't get *Kicker*'s guide so I ended up buying *Bild*'s guide, which was actually even better because it had been produced by the newspaper organising the fantasy football competition I was entering. There were less than ten days left until the start of the league and I had to absorb as much information as possible. I also watched all the videos that I could find on the internet so I could be as certain as possible when choosing my players. The first round of the German Cup and the Super Cup are played before the league starts, and they were excellent games to help in choosing the best possible options.

I could only enter six teams, the maximum number defined by the rules of the contest, which meant I didn't have the huge amount of work that it took to manage my teams in the English league, in which there was no limit to the number of teams you could enter. I loved the fact that each competitor could only have six teams, it meant that we could all go toe-to-toe and see who the best player was. My strategy was to build my teams based on blocks from each club; for example, one team would have the Bayern Munich defenders and Borussia Dortmund forwards, and the other would have the opposite. There was also a limit of only three players per club, a rule similar to the competition in England. However, the best rule of the competition was that we had to pick not just 11 players, but build a squad of 18, and each week we had to choose 11 players from the 18 that were part of the squad. This introduced an extra component that made it more like being a real coach – excellent! It would need dedication and excellent decision-making every single week of the competition. The players' prices were also based on the official website *transfermarkt.com*, the official website, which gave a more realistic edge to the competition.

Friday, 24 August 2012

The Bundesliga started with a clash between Borussia Dortmund, the defending champions, and Werder Bremen, a German club with a great tradition and history. I was completely prepared and satisfied with my final choices. Strategically, there was no chance of success without choosing some players from Bayern Munich and Borussia Dortmund, the two best teams and favourites for the title, but Bayern's best players, such as Robben or Ribery, were so expensive that it was hard to justify picking them because they would use up so much of the budget. That's why I didn't pick the big stars. The remaining players in my squad were from clubs that I thought would have a good season, such as Bayer Leverkusen, or players who had a good price and that I thought would stand out, such as Alex Meier of Eintracht Frankfurt. The rules stipulated that there could only be substitutions in January, during the winter market, just like the real league.

In addition to the points scored when the player scores, assists or doesn't concede (in the case of goalkeepers and defenders), there was also an evaluation of each player's performance by journalists, as well as statistical data on challenges won. I thought these rules were great because, for example, a defensive midfielder who didn't score goals could still be a good choice as he would get a bonus if he won more than 60 per cent of his challenges! This made the competition much fairer and more interesting than the equivalent in England, where no one would select an average player such as Claude Makelele or Nicky Butt. That meant every competitor had to study every player, not just the guys who scored goals or made the most assists. It's interesting that it was an English company who produced and sold this game to a German newspaper, but I have never seen such a well-thought-out fantasy football game in England.

After the first set of fixtures were played, I felt some disappointment with the position I was in. The team that would become my strongest were positioned in 81,707th place. That was slightly above the middle of the table. In the English game, I was used to starting much better and having a good position after the first week, but in Germany I had to be patient and draw up a half-season strategic plan, because, according to my model, there would be players who would not start well, but who could perform well over the whole period before the winter break. On day two, I started to rise up the table, and my best team was now in 40,671st place, which was a bit of a relief. And on day three I was already up to 13,888th place. I know all these numbers because I have kept all the emails that the competition organisers sent at the end of each week. By the end of the seventh week, at the beginning of October, I was in 2,074th place, having gone up every week, which showed that I was using the right strategy.

On a personal level, during that season, I had to make some very important decisions away from the pitch – me and Patricia decided that it was the right time to have a baby. The timing was good because even if she became pregnant soon, our future child wouldn't be born until the end of the German league, so my concentration wouldn't be disrupted. I also decided to go to England to take a level one intensive course in football coaching. Since I was a teenager, I'd always thought I could be a great coach. I remember organising the teams when I played in high school. I was usually the captain and the guy who came up with the strategy and tactics. Now I had the time and the money to go to another country and get my coaching badges – the system in Portugal is pretty bad and slow – so, why not?

The course was run in October at the Hampshire Football Association. I took a week off work and travelled to England. The course was terrific, and I finished with a pass, returning to Portugal with the certificate. The tutor was Jon Gittens, a former player who played for some good English teams like Southampton and Middlesbrough. I remember another guy on the course, who was older than me, saying goodbye and telling me, out of nowhere, that I was 'a brave man', probably for having the courage to go to England to take the course. I have never forgotten those words.

It was at a hotel in Basingstoke, England, when I set up my team for the German league matchday of the week, and curiously it went amazingly well. When I returned to Portugal, I was in 359th place! I felt great, the coaching course complete and a great 'Super Manager' performance – happy days. The only time I didn't go up in the table was between the 10th and 11th round of fixtures; instead, I went down from 42nd to 68th. But on day 12 I reached a new high: I won the 'Manager of the Week' award, having scored the same points as another competitor, and I won my first prize in Germany – a fantastic electric shaver that I still use today! I managed to get the prize through German friends of my in-laws as I gave their address to the *Bild* management, then they send it on to me in Portugal. But more important than that, my overall ranking was now third! Everything was going smoothly with my teams – when a player was banned or injured, I still had a great option on the bench and moved the player into my starting 11. Even one of the cheapest players in my squad, Jens Langeneke of Fortuna Dusseldorf, was doing well! By week 13 I was up to second, and in week 14 I finally took the lead! What a fantastic feeling! I was flying high and loving everything about the game.

What would happen now? Would I have enough skill to keep first place? There were still four weeks to go before the end of the first half of the season, and the title of winter champion, for which the prize was a car (a Suzuki Swift), was perfectly within my reach. I kept the lead in the following weeks and entered the 17th and final week before the winter break with no one above me. The set-up of my team was based on Bayern Munich defenders, such as Boateng or Dante, and a midfield made up of Dortmund players, such as Blacszczykowski or Mario Gotze, as well as striker Lewandowski. Leverkusen was also a good choice, with Lars Bender and Kiessling standing out. Players from mid-table teams, such as Noveski from Mainz, Meier from Frankfurt and Nils Petersen from Bremen, were also doing well. My team's name was 'WiederaufLieben3', which meant 'Return to Life', named after the disappointment and troubled season I had had the year before in the English fantasy football competition. Looking back, the name seems like a bit of an exaggeration, but it certainly shows how I felt. My nickname was 'kickrem', because 'rem' are my initials, Rui Esteves Marques, and 'kick' because one of my first successful teams in England was called 'My Kick'. I have adopted this nickname to register and write in fantasy football forums these days.

The vital game of the last day ended up being Hoffenheim vs Dortmund on 16 December 2012. For my rivals, it would be good if Dortmund didn't concede a goal because they had players like goalkeeper Weidenfeller or defenders like Piszczek or Hummels. But I also had players from Dortmund – Lewandowski and the young German Mario Gotze, who could make all the difference for me. When Gotze scored in the 26th minute with a brilliant shot from outside the area, I started to think I could win. The result of 3-1 to Dortmund was perfect for me! Besides Gotze's goal, Lewandowski had also scored! I was guaranteed my second title of the season. I was the winter champion! What a great end to 2012! The *Bild* newspaper asked me for a photo and an interview. But I was a bit disappointed that the article in the newspaper was much smaller than I expected. They wrote a bit about me and used some quotes from the interview, but there wasn't a photo.

There was a competition gap of almost a month after that, which gave me more than enough time to think about the replacements that I could make once the transfer window opened. As I was in the lead, I could adopt a more defensive structure, in strategic terms. I thought I was risking too much by not having a defensive element from Dortmund, and I also decided that I should try to free up some budget from the subs to buy in a third element from Bayern, who was not as expensive as their main stars but was having a good season nonetheless – Toni Kroos. I bought Weidenfeller, the goalkeeper from Dortmund, and Stranzl, plus Arango from Borussia Monchengladbach. I had to drop Mario Gotze – I couldn't afford to be emotional even though he had been so important in my success so far that season – I had to find money to be able to put in Kroos from the Bavarian team. Defender Martin Stranzl was playing impressively in the challenges, almost always getting three extra points because he was winning more than 60 per cent of them in almost every game. Juan Arango was also a consistent regular, and his quality versus the price meant it was a particularly high-risk change. I thought through all these moves very carefully; I couldn't make a wrong decision because there was no chance to change the squad after that.

In January 2013, with my fantasy football season hitting such a high note, I decided to enrol in a scouting course that had been organised by a Portuguese company who were offering a very interesting reward to the five best students – an internship in the scouting department in a Portuguese Premier League club: Sporting Clube de Portugal or Estoril Praia. I have some interesting memories from the course: sometimes the classes coincided with the beginning of the German league matches and I had to take my laptop with me because at lunch time the team line-ups would be released and I had to focus on selecting my 11 for that weekend. After that I would go back to my classes. When I think of those days, I am proud of my discipline and ability to organise my time, managing to succeed in several areas at the same time.

Analysing what I learned during the scouting course, I can't say it was particularly good in terms of content, but it had been positive because of the networking opportunity, and it gave me an initial idea about the scouting market in Portugal. The final piece of work, which would determine the best five students, consisted of a report about an under-19 match between Sporting and Benfica, played in the world-famous sporting academy at Alcochete, where players like Cristiano Ronaldo, Nani and Quaresma started their careers. Alternatively, you could opt to watch another game from the Portuguese league between Sporting and FC Porto on television and produce a report from it. I thought carefully before I started, but in the end I thought that the judges would value the report more if I wrote it on the under-19 match because I had to drive more than 50 miles to see the game. It was more like a true scouting mission – rather than watching a game on TV in the comfort of your own home. From the 40 students, only eight chose this option, so I thought maybe I would have an advantage. All I had to do now was give it my all and do the best job possible. So, on 2 March 2013, I went to the match with my brother Sérgio – he came with me to record the game on video just in case I needed to review anything before submitting my final report, while I focussed on the match. It was a lively game, and very well played. I took my notes and absorbed all the information I needed to produce the report. Sporting won the game 3-2, and I chose Daniel Podence of Sporting as the man of the match. From Benfica, I chose Bernardo Silva as the best player from the team. Today, around five years later, these two players both have very good careers: Podence was part of the Sporting first team, playing a good number of matches as a starter, and he is now at Olympiakos in Greece, and Bernardo Silva plays for the powerful Manchester City, having an important role at the team, after conquering the French league with Monaco.

I waited patiently for the report assessments, confident that I would be one of the best five and would earn my first contact in professional football at Sporting or Estoril. But I wasn't! I didn't make the top five. It was disappointing and difficult to take. I have read two of the reports that were selected as the best, and I'm still not convinced. Anyway, I started to question myself – was I overrating myself as a potential scout? My answer was clear – I was good enough to succeed. After accepting this unfair rejection, I had to look forward and stay focussed on the other great challenge in my life – the *Bild* 'Super Manager' competition.

The second half of the season in Germany was already halfway through when I finished the course, and I had kept my lead. My level of consistency was impressive week after week. On 30 March 2013, Bayern won 9-2 against Hamburg and my three Bayern players received high scores, another memorable moment for me. But days later I suffered a blow – Toni Kroos suffered a serious injury in a Champions League match and was declared out for the rest of the season. I had to carry on the competition with one less player until the end, and he was one of the most expensive players in my squad. I had to stay strong and keep calm.

With seven weeks to go I could make it as I was leading with a substantial points advantage, and, apart from Kroos, only Langeneke from Dusseldorf had fitness issues. Bayern and Dortmund were also having a great run in the Champions League. Sometimes Heynckes and Klopp saved some of the big-name players, but there were some positives; for example, my Polish duo (Lewandowski and Blacszczykovski) from Dortmund came on from the bench and both had a great impact in only 20 minutes on the field. I watched as many of the matches as I could, and I remember how exciting it was to see multiple broadcasts of all the games at 2.30pm, with the report focus switching from game to game as something important happened. Then, with four weeks to go, something weird happened: a complete black out of the *Bild* 'Super Manager' website for the whole weekend. We couldn't follow the changes in the table live, as usual.

When finally, on Monday, the problem was solved, the table was updated, and I found that the second-placed player had cut the gap substantially between us! I remained undeterred, and the next weekend I gained more points than him and restored my higher lead again. I was confident and in control, but on the penultimate week I had a very poor weekend, so everything would be decided on the last set of fixtures.

Saturday, 18 May 2013

The decision day arrived. After 33 weeks of competition, the champion would finally be known. I made my last selections before the start of the last nine matches, which would all be played at the same time. I felt calm and that I had done all the work I could. As in 2010, before the last game of the season in England, I opted not to follow the matches that would decide the final winner. Because of superstition, I decided to watch my *Family Ties* DVD again, as it had worked so well three years before! When the games ended, I used the internet to check the results and the goalscorers. When I saw what had happened at one of the most important matches, Borussia Monchengladbach vs Bayern Munich, I realised that things had gone the way I wanted! After seeing the highlights of the other matches, I knew I was right and that I had increased my advantage and would be the winner. And, yes, I was correct! I had achieved something amazing: a Portuguese guy who knew very little German had won, and against everyone in Germany, with more than 200,000 Germans competing! I felt amazing, and the prize money was very welcome – €100,000! By this time, I already knew that I was going to be a father at the end of the year – my wife was already two months pregnant – and as you can imagine I was over the moon, more good things were happening to me. It is a great responsibility to bring a child into the world, so we waited a bit longer than a lot of couples do, but we were pretty sure that the time was right. When Patricia took the pregnancy test and the result was positive, we both knew our lives were about to enter a new and exciting phase. She was nervous and worried, but I knew she would be a great mother. So, everything was perfect. I had won two major fantasy football competitions in two different countries in just three years and now I was going to be a dad! Nobody can take any of that away from me! Ever!

12

FOOTBALL FANTASY: MY RULES AND TIPS

My fantasy football performances and overall experience are substantial enough that I think I can help others. There is no mathematical formula for being the best and winning. However, there are some useful tips that you can follow to maximise your chances of winning.

To be in first place at the end of a competition, you need to make quite a number of correct decisions. You will not always get it right, but if you make more good decisions than the other competitors, it will be enough to win. And to make good decisions, you must study the relevant factors. These are the main rules you should follow:

Rule number one – Strong pre-season preparation
You need to get as much information as possible about the football arena you will be competing in. One of the most difficult times to get accurate information is during the pre-season. But it's also the most precious information you can get because, before the season starts, you have everything to play for, so if you can apply your knowledge from the start, you could really benefit from it. My rule is that when the pre-season starts for the clubs, it must also start for any

fantasy football competitor. The ideal but perhaps utopic scenario is that you watch all the friendly games and try to understand which players and teams will start the league better. A common mistake I've seen other players make is to underestimate the amount of pre-season thinking you need to do, and think that if you do make errors you will have enough time to fix them. But isn't it better if you start in pole position?

I always started strong in my golden years in England, but my worst year was the one in which I got married in August, the month the competition started. This suggests that I didn't make the necessary pre-season preparations and I missed some vital information, maybe spending more time on the wedding preparations than I should have. In the English game, it was more important to start well because the rules usually allowed substitutions at the end of the first month, so whoever was ahead would have an advantage as they wouldn't have to use their substitutions early on. If you start well it's because you've selected the right players from the beginning, so you can save your substitutions for later in the game, which can be make or break, and if you're on top you can take greater risks later on. In Germany there are official cup matches (in both countries there is also the Super Cup) before the league starts, which helps immensely in making the right decisions. However, the strategy I followed in Germany couldn't only be based on starting well because the first deadline for substitutions wasn't until mid-season, so I had to last for four months instead of one month like in England.

If you do your research well during the pre-season but a player you selected doesn't perform well at the beginning of the competition or gets injured, it doesn't mean that you made a mistake because you don't have a crystal ball to predict the future. But if a certain player you didn't select is playing outstandingly and you know that you didn't pay attention to him before, even if you knew that he had played well for a number of years, it's time to admit that you didn't prepare well enough.

It has been very rare that I have had to admit this, but more recently I tried to play a fantasy football game in the Belgian league and I made a mistake. I didn't have enough knowledge about the league, but I made a good effort to absorb as much information as I could to start well in the competition; however, my results were poor – there is so much information to learn that a guy like me, who only knew around five per cent of the players when I started and hadn't seen a game or even a highlight of a Belgian team for over a decade, couldn't just start playing and win. A player called Jeremy Perbet, who was signed by Charleroi before the competition started, had a terrific season, scoring 24 goals. I didn't know the player or anything about his career before, and I didn't bother to research him, I just ignored him. When I realised that he was a great player, I did the research and found that he had played two seasons in the Spanish league, scoring a number of goals in each, and in Belgium before that, and he was one of the most prolific goal scorers for five seasons in a row. How can I complain about my poor results in Belgium? I didn't do the research, so I clearly deserved to fail.

The bottom line is you can control the level of research you do before the season starts and you need to spend the required time to absorb all the information available. If you don't have this attitude you will have no excuses if you fail later.

Rule number two – Substitutions: discipline and planning

If you want to win a competition that lasts nine months, you must play it like you are running a marathon. And as a marathon runner you need to know at which points you will find the hydration stations. For fantasy football players, substitutions are like water, so you need to study the rules of the competition and understand the times when you can make them.

If you are playing a game with defined transfer windows, it's important to plan a team up to the point when you will be allowed to make changes. If you can only change your team after 17 matches, you can't make a plan based on the first five weeks. It doesn't matter if the players you pick will have a tough first few weeks at the start, you need to plan for the whole period before the transfer window opens. So, it's important not to fall into the temptation of attacking straight away by putting in players who have an easier initial schedule because in the medium term this could be a bad thing, as you can't replace them until later in the season.

If the game rules allow you to make transfers from the beginning of the competition, you must be careful and disciplined about the substitutions you make. You need to create your own criteria. I have played games with only six subs allowed in the whole season and at any time from the start of the competition. It's tough to resist, but you can't risk being without subs when you need them. If a player is out for two or three weeks, I probably wouldn't substitute him too early. I always try to work to the following rule: the percentage of subs left must be at least the same as or higher than the percentage of weeks left until the competition finishes. If I have broken this rule in the past, it has been because I'm in trouble and looking like I'm going to lose. I end up breaking the rule and taking risks, but it doesn't pay off. Although, if I have a lot of players who have long-term injuries I have to change them; I can't keep them just because I'll break my percentage rule if I don't. If you've read the story of my best seasons in England, you will have concluded that I made some mistakes, particularly at the end of the season. But in the season I won, my subs were so spot on that I beat the perfect team, as I explained in chapter nine.

When you are playing a short-term competition like a monthly or a World Cup/Euro tournament, you have to be even more wise because you have much less time to decide when the best time to make a substitution is. I didn't have much success in recent competitions like these, but not because of a lack of discipline when using subs. To win a Euro or a World Cup tournament, you have to guess who will be the champions before making your team decisions. I did well in the World Cup 2006 because Italy was my bet to win from the beginning. But in the more recent World Cup my pick was Argentina and in the European tournament I was more Italy and Germany than Spain or Portugal. I know lots of people who use most of their subs in the first few days in this kind of competition, just to be in the lead. It's crazy and it doesn't work, and they are then left hoping for a miracle.

The most difficult part of managing subs can happen when you're not thinking clearly and don't follow your plan or keep your self-discipline. This links neatly to the next rule.

Rule number three – Keep your cool and focus on your team

As with everything in our lives, I believe we make better decisions when we are able to think things through carefully. Sometimes in the fantasy football world you have to think very fast and decide quickly, so you need to keep a clear and cool head all the time. This is most important when you are on a deadline to choose players or make substitutions. I consider myself to be a well-balanced person, but I am only human, and I have my flaws and crazy moments. I have made wrong substitutions in the past when my scores were disappointing and I couldn't stay calm. I lost my cool and wasn't patient enough, but I was able to manage my emotions better after some of those errors and bad experiences. One good skill I have that has been important to my success is my ability to filter out my day-to-day problems, like work issues, and completely forget them whilst working on my fantasy football teams.

One of the things I often did, and I would recommend to others, was read inspirational books to help me keep a steady head when things were not going my way. Apart from the Nigel Mansell book I have already referred to, I have other favourites in my library, mostly autobiographies of successful tennis players, from Sampras to Agassi or McEnroe. It's a sport that requires a balanced mind, and managing your emotions is also key. I really believe that Roger Federer would make a fantastic fantasy football player because of his ability to stay focussed. I even bought a book of tips on how to make your brain function better, and I have started to follow some of the advice, like eating blueberries, for example. When I had to make big decisions,

I would buy them to eat a day before decision day. It may sound a bit weird but it usually worked.

It's not only your mind that you have to keep balanced, it's also your team! When I started my 'You The Manager' career, I was quite naïve and I remember creating a team with three strikers, Alan Shearer, Thierry Henry and Ruud van Nistelrooy. There was no doubt about the power of my attacking line, but my team were poor and didn't perform well. Why? Because a fantasy football team that is constructed well in terms of budget versus player prices will create a balanced team in every area: defence, midfield and attack. You can't select the three best strikers and hope for success because your budget will then only allow you to play with a weak defensive line or a poor midfield. I remember having two Crystal Palace midfielders and one of their defenders in my team; it was ridiculous. I have never played in a Spanish league fantasy football competition, but I don't think the best team could contain Cristiano Ronaldo (when he was at Real Madrid), Lionel Messi and Antoine Griezmann, for example. It doesn't make sense, even though Ronaldo and Messi are two of the best players that football has ever produced. Another common error people make is selecting players they think are underrated. You may find that they are underrated and you are right, but you should be careful when choosing players because like this what you think is a 'bargain' will often become 'expensive' if he loses you points.

One of the essential skills of a good fantasy football player is to know which players are overrated, as it can be disastrous to your team if you don't spot them. If you do choose them, again it will mean you have an unbalanced team. You must have a good, balanced team in terms of budget if you are going to stand any chance of winning, which actually applies to the real football world as well: everybody knows that the Brazilian team from the World Cup in 1982 was probably the best in the competition's history in terms of midfield and attack, but their defence was weak, and a more balanced Italian team knocked them out of the tournament. I'm an old romantic and I always like to see the more attacking teams win, but I'm more realistic if I'm playing fantasy football – I have to remember that balance is key. When I won in Germany one of the comments on the forum for the competition said my team were 'nothing special'. I had to laugh; it might not have been anything special but no one in the country could beat it! The team was special because it won, and it won because it was balanced!

Rule number four – Know your strengths and weaknesses

This is a rule that needs some personal reflection. In life, some aspects of our personalities will remain the same, but others will change. Now, I am a very different person to who I was 20 years ago, so I'm also a different fantasy football player. I generally know my skills as a player, but I have to reflect from time to time to see if anything has changed.

My memory is a particularly good asset to me. I remember lots of football facts from throughout the entire history of the beautiful game. When a fantasy football game is launched, I can remember the prices of the players with ease. That allows me to think about possible combinations of players throughout the day, even when I'm doing other things (or at least pretending I am!). It's not uncommon for me to think about my teams when I'm in a supermarket queue or traffic jam, especially if I'm on the verge of making a big decision. I can also memorise lots of information about the next games in the calendar, which helps me with my thoughts.

I'm also a person who was born watching football. Since I was no more than four years old, I've been able to sit down and watch a whole football match without losing my concentration. My passion for the game is unquestionable and undeniable. This is an asset in fantasy football terms. However, sometimes my football knowledge does let me down. A good example I can give you is as follows: I grew up with the memory of Diego Maradona and his terrific Mexico '86 World Cup performance, and I thought that because Lionel Messi had the same profile as Diego that he would win a World Cup in a similar way, so I tend to overrate Argentina and base my decisions too much on these similarities and my emotional connections rather than thinking rationally. If you ask me who will win the next World Cup, I immediately think Argentina, even after my bet on them was wrong in 2010 and 2014. I want to be more neutral and rational in my views, but sometimes I admit I'm not. Once Argentina had been knocked out by France I thought France would win; I was able to make a more rational decision, which was completely correct. So, I know it's important to remember that emotional attachments can be a weakness in fantasy football. I also grew up watching Spain and Portugal lose all the time in crucial games, so I wasn't expecting either team to win the European tournament, but then Spain even won a World Cup. I can be too conventional in my choices and sometimes get it wrong – again because of experience. Some teams seem to really struggle when they lose a lot, but remember that one day they will overcome it, like Spain's golden generation, who were bold enough to win and make history. I didn't predict that, and I'd consider that to have been a weakness (one I still have, but I'm fighting against it).

One strength I know I definitely have is the ability to evaluate a player. I can see quickly if he is good or not and if he is having a good period or not – I will talk about this more in chapter 20. This special ability has been very useful and has helped me profit in fantasy football terms. If I lose this skill, I'm done. As I've mentioned before, I think my evaluation of Gareth Bale back in 2010, which was crucial to my win, is a perfect example of my skill in this area. Everybody knew that Bale was a very good player, but he had already been at Spurs for a number of seasons without success and was no more than another squad player, but I knew that he was close to showing his best and with the help of Harry Redknapp, his coach at the time, I thought it was a sure thing.

Speaking of the coaches, they too can have an influence on my fantasy football team choices, but sometimes I make the mistake of not considering them: I make an assessment of a player, decide he is fantastic and I pick him ... but then I forget to analyse the coach's profile! There are coaches who are too defensive and waste very gifted players by putting them on the bench, choosing other players who are better tactically. There are coaches who do a lot of squad rotation, and in this scenario not even the best players in that team are good fantasy football picks. So, I just want to emphasise this, it's not enough to identify a good player, you have to think about the coach profile as well.

We are always in a constant fight to maintain our strengths and at the same time suppress our weaknesses.

You will be a better fantasy football player if you can assess your own strengths and weaknesses correctly.

Rule number five – Organising, ready to improvise

You must try to optimise your time and energy. There are lots of uncertain things in daily life, but you should try to organise yourself and create some routine to save some time and energy for when you have to think on your feet. This also applies to fantasy football. If I am competing, I try to organise my life well around my fantasy football schedules – as simple as that. When a deadline for subs or starting team decisions is approaching, I make sure I am completely free from other tasks. Sometimes it collides with my professional and personal life, but I have to try to solve any problems in good time before I need to work on my fantasy football teams. A real example of this was when I was competing in the German competition and an important player from my squad was in doubt for that weekend, but the line-ups hadn't been announced and the deadline for selecting your team was approaching. I was online and completely switched off from any other issues, just waiting for the information I needed. When I got it, it confirmed that he was out of the game. So, I benched him and picked another player from my squad, of course. I was leading the table and to my surprise one of my competitors (in Germany we could see each other's teams) kept that player in! It was clear to me that he hadn't been online waiting for confirmation. Maybe he was doing something more interesting or more important to him. I didn't do that though, and it really increased my chances. I'm lucky to have my wife as she is my shield and she frees me from other tasks if I need to focus. I am also lucky to have had the jobs I've had, as I've been able to manage my time and if needed I've been able to take a break to complete my fantasy football tasks. Today, with smartphones, it's even easier. And if I have to travel at tricky times, I plan everything, thinking about when I will find out a line-up or the latest information about whether or not a player has recovered from injury. My fantasy football performance has to be a priority, and if I don't make it so then I can't complain if I lose.

I always try to have different plans for each possible scenario I could be faced with. For example, if player X is not available, I will go with player Y, but if player Y is also out, I will pick player Z. But even if you have thought about all the possible scenarios, there could still be a surprise ahead and you need to be ready to select player W! To make good decisions and to find the right solution, you have to be organised and put the rest of your life on hold to focus and commit to the game. If you think I'm obsessed, I don't care, I just do everything I can to win.

So, to have an efficient and organised plan, you need to find a good source of information, so a reliable website is key. This is worthwhile mentioning because sadly I have lost in the past because of incorrect information. Once I excluded a player from my starting 11 after reading that he was out injured the Friday before, but on the Sunday he actually played, coming on from the bench, and he scored. Imagine my mood after that. So, my advice is to double-check your information.

Rule number six – Perspectives: macro and micro

This is a simple rule that is easy to explain. You should never forget to keep a sense of perspective about the fantasy football competition that you are playing. You can be aware of the best players in a certain team, but if that team is weak or the coach is poor and they are likely to be relegated, you should stay away from picking players from that team. You can apply a micro vision when looking at the best players in a team, but you mustn't forget the macro vision: those players are useless if the team is the weakest in the league because they won't get enough points. Another example is if I choose the best players from a very good team in the league, but I ignore the fact that this team are also playing in another competition, for example the Champions League. The best players will be saved for that other competition, so there is a high probability of rotation within the squad which won't be good for me. It's pretty common to find average teams that have a good season and qualify for the Europa League struggle the next season because they don't have the team structure to play in two competitions that are so demanding in terms of the number of games. So, you must look at the whole picture because if you only focus on a micro perspective you will miss other important factors that can only be spotted if you use a macro perspective.

* * *

ANALYSIS

When you are watching a match, your eyes send information to your brain to help you make decisions. The quality of your interpretation of the information you collect will determine the quality of your decisions. We can control some of the factors that influence this 'interpretation-to-decision' process, but some factors we are born with or at least we only develop after many years of training. What I am trying to say is that there will always be many different outcomes from this process, differing from one person to another, and that will define the performances of each individual in fantasy football or any other competition. This is something we can't control and is built-up based on our life experiences or genetic material. If someone is not interested in football, and doesn't like to watch it or play it, they can't be a good fantasy football player. These are simple and logical assumptions, but it's good to point out that you shouldn't expect to wake up one day, decide you want to be a fantasy football champion and expect to win if you don't have the basics.

But if you follow the rules and tips I have written here, I am pretty sure you will become a better player.

PART III:
FANTASY BECOMES REALITY

13

THE RIGHT TIME

June 2013

So, what now? What should be the next step in my life? At 33 years old, and after winning two major fantasy football competitions, I started to wonder if I could work in the world of professional football? Would someone look at me, realise that I have something special and see me as a potential asset? My CV was looking good and had some very distinct skills on it, but was now the right time to try? After thinking through all these questions, I decided to go ahead. It was time to introduce myself to a professional club and try to get into the football industry. I was much stronger than I had been in 2011, when I'd tried to deliver a portfolio to André Villas-Boas more than once without success. I started to focus on this new aim, and through LinkedIn I began to develop a network of contacts so I could put myself forward as a candidate to work for a club.

One of the first interesting messages I received was from a director of scouting for a club from an English championship team. He set me a challenge to recommend five young Portuguese players who I predicted would have bright futures and good career progression. But after so many years of intense focus on the German and English leagues, my Portuguese football knowledge was not the best. The five players I suggested were players that, if I could go back with the greater knowledge and experience I have now, I wouldn't have picked, for sure (although some of them are actually having a good career).

At that time, I also started to email Portuguese clubs near the city where I lived – Lisbon – telling them my story and emphasising the money I had won, because if I didn't I was usually ignored. The first club that contacted me for an interview were a third-tier club from Sintra, called 1° Dezembro. I was very nervous. When I knocked the door of the room where the meeting was to be held, there was no answer at all! When I came back home, my wife asked me about the interview and I told her what happened. I had been so anxious for nothing. Patricia told me not to be upset and that one day I would laugh at this story. She was right. Some days later, I received a response from Estoril Praia – a team that was riding high with a recent fifth-place finish in the top flight. They asked for my CV, which gave me a good feeling. A few days later, I started sending emails to clubs in Northern Portugal. Very quickly, and surprisingly, FC Porto replied inviting me for an interview. I couldn't believe my luck, my first interview with a club in the first division would be with the champions – in 2013 FC Porto had celebrated their third title in a row, 'the Tri'. I travelled by train to meet with the club scout. While I was waiting to meet him, the charismatic president of the club, Jorge Nuno Pinto da Costa, appeared and said, 'Good afternoon'. This chance meeting turned out to be the most memorable moment of my trip to Porto. The interview went OK and at the end the scout told me that they would be in touch in a few months, but I never heard from them. Ironically, FC Porto didn't win the championship again until five years later and the scouting department had to be restructured after that, with that guy I met leaving for a French team. When I was travelling back home I asked myself, since I'm a Benfica supporter, how would I feel if a rival club hired me? The easy answer was that I would serve this club with the utmost dedication and forget about any emotional ties. I should imagine this is the same for all players, coaches or directors who are supporters of a different club. They all manage to work past it.

From all the feedback I got from clubs overseas, I was really happy with what I received from Kerry Zavagnin, assistant coach of MLS club Sporting Kansas City, and a person with great prestige as a former USA national team player. At the time, I had no idea that fantasy football was something highly valued in America, with a huge following and no doubt an industry that generated millions – although it was based on American football, not soccer. Now I know that baseball, ice hockey and basketball are also big in American fantasy markets. Me and Kerry exchanged some messages, and I realised that he thought very highly of Portuguese football, and I decided to follow Sporting Kansas City and try to watch all of their games. Some of their players at the time had played in Portugal and Spain and the head coach was Peter Vermes, who had played in the Italia '90 World Cup and whose name I remember well from my childhood, either from the sticker collection or from the computer games.

After a few days of frustration from a lack of replies, I got an email from Pedro Bessa, chief scout for Estoril Praia, inviting me for an interview and to watch a game with him at the stadium afterwards in the Europa League play-off against Hapoel Ramat Gan from Israel. I was so happy! Estoril Praia is a club from a beautiful region in Portugal called Estoril near Cascais, a city very well known as a touristic attraction. Portugal Formula 1 Grand Prix was usually at Estoril race track, that is the best in Portugal. The club was founded in 1939 and counts with more than 20 presences in Portugal top division, despite some ups and downs. The club was now living a golden era with more stability and the 2012/2013 season fourth place was the best from the club for more than 60 years! Playing a European competition for the first time was the cherry on top.

But later I learned that the interview would be delayed because Pedro had to travel, but I still went to the match feeling like I could have a future at Estoril. The final result was 0-0 and I recall that in the 73rd minute Gerso, the young Estoril winger, came on and the crowd were excited, hoping that he could help them win the game. I didn't know it at the time but Gerso would be so important to my career. Estoril won the second leg at Israel and faced FC Pasching in the next round, a team from Austria who were easily beaten. The club qualified for the Europa League group stage, which was a tremendous achievement.

Friday, 30 August 2013

In the end, the interview was finally rescheduled on my fifth wedding anniversary. Was it a good omen for a future marriage? Pedro Bessa was a former professional player who put in some good appearances for Gil Vicente and Vitória Guimarães at the peak of his career, playing as a right-back. It was a Friday and a busy day in the finance department at work as we were closing the accounts for the month, but I still managed to leave and get to the Estoril stadium in good time. I introduced myself and used the same strategy that I had in the previous two interviews, and it went really well. I thought I could have a real chance. A few days later I got a phone call from Pedro to say he had spoken to the director of football, Mário Branco, and they wanted me to work for them as a scout! I could start the next weekend! I was so happy, I felt that a new door had opened. I was starting my career as a scout at a very good level with a club who were riding high after their recent qualification for the Europa League. It didn't matter that I was just a volunteer and wouldn't receive any financial compensation. My priority wasn't making money, I just wanted to show my value, and I knew that I still had a lot to learn. The results and recognition would hopefully follow because I believed in my talent and I knew that I had something special to offer. It was game on for me!

However, with this new role on the horizon, it had become impossible for me to defend my title in the *Bild* 'Super Manager' competition. There were no monetary prizes anymore and the rules had changed for the worse. Even with many protests from the usual competitors, the organisation's strange ideas prevailed and the competition began its path to extinction the following season. I thought to myself that I had been lucky to have enjoyed playing the game when it was good, and I was the last champion of the competition. We'll never really know why the changes were made. Nevertheless, my focus had changed, and I was working in football for real.

Patricia completely understood that the time I had been spending on my fantasy football career would now be shifted to the real football world. She knew my goal was to prove my value working for a club, and she believed I could do it. At the time she was more focussed on becoming a mum as she was six months pregnant and starting the countdown to his arrival. My ultimate goal was clear: I wanted to win some new competitions! I had to retire from fantasy football at my peak, but a new era was beginning for me and there were many exciting possibilities ahead. I would need to give my best, as always, and grab the opportunities, but I was sure I could succeed in this new chapter of my life.

14

ESTORIL PRAIA 2013/14
(my first season)

I was ready but nervous at the start of my new career. I had been emailed confirmation of my first live match as a scout: Mafra vs Caldas in the third tier – also known as the National Championships. Pedro also sent me the report template to use for my observations, which consisted of four pages: page one for the team sheets, formation and the main facts like goals and disciplinary actions; page two and three for a short commentary on the performance of each player; and page four, the most important, to highlight the players who were the best in the game and the analysis of their performance, which had to be more detailed.

Sunday, 8 September 2013
I went to Mafra for my first game – a day I will never forget! I made my preparations for the game, collecting information about the expected starting 11 of both teams. I took a notepad and wrote down anything that I thought would be relevant to my report. It was not a very dynamic game and it ended up being decided in the 92nd minute after a set piece that ended in a headed goal, with Mafra winning 1-0. I wrote my report and delivered it as requested

during the week. I received some praise from Pedro: 'for a first time, it's really interesting'. It gave me confidence that I could perform well in my new job. In the following weeks, I continued my work steadily with a scouting mission every weekend. Whenever my games didn't coincide with those of Estoril, I would also watch my team play. This was very important to help me understand which potential new players could fit into our system. This was all new to me but I was loving it.

In mid-October we had the first scouting department meeting, organised by Pedro and with Mário Branco, director of football, also present. I also met the other scouts. In the north, there was Pedro and another colleague, and in the south it was me and three others, two of them being the guys who'd won the role through the scouting course. The meeting began with Mário describing the Estoril squad and explaining the decisions behind each player. Then a scout could give his opinion if he wanted to. I felt good explaining my ideas and it was something I felt comfortable doing. In the end we got a big surprise: our coach Marco Silva came to meet and greet us. Since the first time I saw him speak at a press conference on TV, I thought he would have a great future as a coach, and I was not mistaken. He eventually left Estoril at the end of the season, signing for top team Sporting. He managed to reach the English Premier League and he is the Everton manager at the time of writing – after being at Watford and Hull City and becoming champion in Greece with Olympiakos. I haven't met him again since then, but if I ever do meet him again he probably won't remember me. I would've liked to get to know him better as I think we'd have got along, but timing and luck was not in my favour.

I continued my work with determination, always focussing on the second and third-tier matches in Portugal. For a club like Estoril Praia, it was a good strategy to seek out young talents in the lower levels who might have the ability to step up and play in the top division. I quickly became an expert in this type of talent spotting and was efficient at filtering out the players who had the potential to play at a higher level. I saw some remarkable games in those first few months; for example, a Portuguese Cup match between Cova da Piedade (third division) and Gil Vicente (first division), which lasted for 120 minutes without any goals and it was decided on penalties. I also saw our first-ever home game in the UEFA Europa League group stage against powerful Sevilla (who won the trophy later that season). We lost 2-1 but it was a great match.

Pedro also used to send me players to analyse via Wyscout – a huge database of football matches – with an emphasis on the French second division, Ligue 2, which was an excellent source for scouting. In addition to the matches he sent me to, I also started to watch other teams' matches online when players I liked to follow were in the squad, such as Angers, Nancy or Tours. We were on the verge of selling our main striker, Luís Leal, and we needed to find a substitute, so our focus was on this position. The player I liked the most and strongly backed was Andy Delort from Tours, but it was extremely difficult to convince Traffic – the company that controlled and managed Estoril – to invest. Another player who we both loved was a Haitian player, Jeff Louis, from Nancy, who would fit nicely in to our system if we eventually sold our star Evandro. Today, looking back, it seems that me and Pedro were too dreamy and ambitious, but we were doing a good job.

On a personal level, another great day finally arrived; the birth of my son Leonardo on Friday, 6 December. I was sure everything would go according to plan so I don't remember being nervous. I wanted to be there for Patricia all the way through to support her as much as I could. As I had been expecting, my life entered a whole new dimension and my sense of responsibility greatly increased. Since then my number-one goal in life is to be the best father I can and to make Leonardo happy.

The day after Leonardo was born, Sporting Kansas City reached the final of the Major League Soccer (MLS) championship. I watched the game on my own at home, while my wife and son were still in hospital, and I was happy to see them crowned champions for the second time in their history. The player who scored the equaliser in the final match, Aurélien Collin, a central defender, had played in Portugal at Vitória, so maybe I had given them some positive energy! I congratulated Kerry on the win.

Eight days after that, I returned to my scouting duties and watched another third-tier match. Estoril's season was going well, and on 16 December I went to see our win against Gil Vicente, and we clinched fourth place in the league, just behind the big three (Benfica, Sporting and FC Porto). It was a very demanding period for me with my new role as a father, and it would be an understatement to say I was exhausted, but I couldn't stop my work as a scout because I had to make the most of the opportunity I had at Estoril and the transfer window was just around the corner. We had to reinforce our attack because, as expected, we had lost Luís Leal to a team from the Middle East, and I wanted to put forward some suggestions for a good alternative. I was on paternity leave from my day job and was at home for a month, so I took advantage of my free time when Leonardo was sleeping to watch as many online matches as possible. From Romania to Peru, Bulgaria or Turkey, I was watching everything and taking notes on players I spotted to send to Pedro. Looking back, I don't think I was under as much pressure as I thought I was, and I should have helped my wife a bit more, but my choice was to watch football. I was so determined to have a career in football that it was hard to stop, but she understood and has always supported me.

My first transfer window as a scout ended with some disappointment. Estoril didn't strengthen the attack that January, making an unambitious move to recall a player who was out on loan to a second division team instead. It was the first time I felt frustration as a scout, but it was nothing major. Anyway, I did what I had to do, worked on what I could and suggested some options, such as Wilmar Jordan, a Colombian striker who was in Bulgaria, and Raul Ruidiaz, a young promising Peruvian. I remember recommending Rithely, a Brazilian player I saw in the second division in Brazil, and the now famous N'Golo Kanté, who was playing for Caen at the time, fighting to be promoted to Ligue 1. But my most spectacular discovery at this time was a kid I saw playing for Istres in the French second division called Naby Keita. Istres were a team in crisis at the bottom of the table, but he caught my attention in a game against Lens. I have some emails saved from that period, and here are some of my thoughts from my reports to Pedro: on 23 December I reported that he had a 'phenomenal game, could recover the ball and start the attacking moves with quality', and on 7 March I wrote 'he will only stop at Juventus or Chelsea, the more I see him, the more I am convinced'. And now we know where he is and how much market value he has. This kind of experience boosted my confidence.

One Saturday morning in the February, my brother Sérgio called me out of the blue to say that he was in the gym and Benfica president Luís Filipe Vieira was doing some exercises only a few metres away from him. He offered to try and speak to him about me if I wanted him to. Of course, I said yes. After talking to my brother, he showed an interest in meeting me and gave him his personal email address, telling him that I should send my CV and a cover letter! I did it a few days later, and the reply was brief: his adviser emailed me to invite me for lunch at Estádio da Luz with the director of the Benfica training centre, Armando Jorge Carneiro, and the president. I felt nervous but excited, and I even bought a red tie for the occasion. However, two days before I was due to go, one of the club's famous names, Mário Coluna, tragically died. When I arrived at the club's training centre in Seixal two days after, I already knew the president had left to go to Mozambique for the funeral, but Armando Jorge Carneiro was still going to meet me. Then I was informed that he was in a long meeting and I would be met by two other members of the club's team instead. It was terrible news, and the meeting didn't go very well. I never received an official answer from the club.

So I turned my attention back to the summer transfer window. I had four months to go, during which time I would need to see as many games as possible to absorb as much information as I could. As the season continued, I consolidated my knowledge of the second and third tiers of the Portuguese league. Some names on my list started to emerge as possible players for Estoril the following season. The strongest candidate from the third tier was a young forward from Torreense – João Vieira. I had seen him play a few times, improving his performance in each game, and Pedro, who lived in the north near the Porto region, also decided to come and watch him play. On 16 March 2014, Vieira's team Torreense beat Fatima 3-1 and he scored a hat-trick! He had a terrific game and Pedro was convinced of his ability. From the players I followed in the third tier, he was the most consistent and the best choice. He had been dismissed by Marítimo, a club who used to sign a number of young up-and-coming players, which could have led us to be suspicious about him, but I thought that people always make mistakes so they could have missed him, and we had to take advantage whenever that happened. I remember a similar situation when Deco, a player who never got an opportunity in the first team at SL Benfica, was dismissed, but FC Porto signed him and he became one of the best midfielders in the world, winning two Champions League Finals – one with FC Porto and another with Barcelona.

The season was continuing to go well for Estoril. We were in the fight for a place in the European competitions again. It was difficult to reach the top three, but after winning against Braga in February and Guimarães in April, we were close to the precious fourth place.

As the season was coming to a close, I was excited to know if any of the players I had recommended in my final work would be signed. I had delivered my 'shadow teams' from the second and third tiers in mid-May, based on the two or three best possible players for each position according to my assessments throughout the season. The best teams in the second division that season had been Moreirense and Penafiel, so some of the players in the shadow teams were from those clubs, of course. But players from teams that had won promotion would already have a good chance of playing in the first tier, so I thought my scouting report would be more useful if I suggested players from teams that would be staying in the second division. I recommended a total of 30 players, two for each defensive position and three for each midfield and attack positions. Estoril wanted to invest in young players to boost the club's finances by selling them at a higher price later, so the players I put forward couldn't be any older than 27. Today, more than four years after I delivered this report, it's very interesting to see where they are now. I am proud to say that 60 per cent of those players are enjoying successful careers and play at a level higher than they were then. Below are the five highlights:

MIKA – goalkeeper – had two solid seasons at Boavista in Portugal in the first tier and then signed for Sunderland, although it was maybe a step too far for him.

PAULINHO – right-back – he is well established in Portugal's first division and even had experience at SC Braga, but came back to Chaves.

ANDRÉ SIMÕES – central midfielder – he is in his third consecutive season at AEK Athens (Greece), and is one of the more influential players in the team, helping them to win the Greek league in 2017/18.

ANDRÉ SOUSA – central midfielder – completely established in the first division, with lots of assists and goals for Belenenses. He was transferred in the summer of 2018 to Sporting Gijon from Spain and played in the Europa League two seasons ago.

RICARDO VALENTE – winger/striker – one of the best Marítimo players, he is a regular for them every season and they are usually fighting for Europa League qualification in the Portuguese first division.

* * *

However, my first moment of real pride in my career came when I saw my work bear fruit with the good news that Estoril were about to sign two of the players from the group of 30 that I had recommended:

ANDERSON ESITI – he is a young and strong Nigerian defensive midfielder from Leixões. The first time I saw him play live I was very impressed, and he was my number-one player in my report. He was good at recovering the ball, dominating in the midfield challenges and technically he was OK, making quality long passes. I stated that for his age (only 19 at the time) he had everything he needed to progress and be a top player. Today he is playing for Gent in the Belgian first division.

KUCA – he is a winger from Cape Verde who I watched a lot on video, and although Chaves didn't achieve promotion, he made some remarkable performances during the championship, showing he was good enough to play at a higher level. I liked his unpredictable moves and attacking skills; he could dribble and assist with efficiency, but he could also score goals with great finishes. Estoril sold him after only half a season to a Turkish team, making a very good profit, but he came back to Portugal after struggling to adapt.

I should have felt happy because the Estoril squad was going to have two players that I had recommended playing for them next season, but even so I was still not satisfied. I have a characteristic that I find difficult to manage sometimes – I always want more and I find it hard to deal with my feelings when I think that the decisions made are wrong. A young player named Afonso Taira from Atletico, who I had watched at least five times during the season and never highlighted him, was also signed. For me, he lacked certain attributes that I think are important for a midfield player: he needed to play at a higher tempo and be more aggressive in his challenges for loose balls. On the day of the final season meeting, I criticised his signing vehemently but was too direct. But it's my style and sometimes I can't contain myself. I was also somewhat frustrated that none of the young players I suggested from the third tier had been hired. Today, Afonso Taira is in the Israeli Premier League.

My first season as a scout was over. It was quite intense and challenging, having watched 34 games live and in my opinion the reports I had delivered were very good. Pedro, the chief scout must have agreed with me because in June he told me that he was counting on me for the next season. He said he had already told Mário Branco that I should continue. I hoped I would continue and that people liked my work, but I made it clear that I could not continue without any financial compensation. I had shown my value and they knew what I could offer, so it didn't make sense for me to do it for free anymore. I think we should be humble in life and starting from the bottom shouldn't be a problem, but knowing how much Estoril Praia had generated in transfer revenue and the money paid to players and other people on the staff, I felt I should be paid as well, it was only fair.

Personally, it had been a tough period. Some people had warned me that I wasn't going to be able to handle my full-time job as well as my part-time role in football, plus the extra pressure of being a first-time father. The fact is, I made it to the summer of 2014 tired but successful, and doing well on all three fronts.

15

ESTORIL PRAIA 2014/15 (second season)

I watched the 2014 World Cup while waiting for the start of my second season at Estoril in August. Pedro hinted that I would continue, and I was to be paid now, but I had to wait for the budget decisions for confirmation. I don't remember for sure, but I think I had asked for €300 per month to continue, but if they offered me less I would still accept.

Then out of the blue, I received an email from Pedro that hit me like a ton of bricks! He said that they couldn't fulfil my request for payment and that my time at Estoril was over. To help you understand the impact this had on me, I can remember exactly where I was when I read it – I was in the Paço de Arcos health centre and I think my son was having a vaccination that day – I told my wife the news and I remember the disappointment. So, what now? I had no plan B, I had spent the last couple of months thinking that staying at Estoril was the best option for me and that I was going to get the financial reward I deserved. I felt used. When I gave my best and worked very hard at fantasy football, I always managed to achieve results, but it felt like in real football my prize was to be kicked out. I tried to stay calm and not lose my cool. It was difficult, but I managed to find some positives in the situation. I told Pedro that I was very disappointed with the decision but asked him for two things: to add a positive recommendation for me on LinkedIn and to authorise me to write an email to Mário Branco telling my story and asking for advice. My requests were accepted. Pedro wrote me a nice recommendation and I wrote to Mário.

I held my head high and started looking for a new job. I told the whole story to Kerry Zavagnin, the assistant coach at Sporting Kansas City, who promptly answered me, suggesting that maybe it was a good time for me to fly to Kansas City and meet the club! I decided to go; it was my best chance to find a new club, so I had to take the risk. I planned a trip at the beginning of October, and I still had a few days' leave to take from my full-time job.

However, there was another twist in the tale. I was at home after a usual day at work in August, and I realised that I had left my mobile phone in the car – something I never did. When I picked it up, I noticed that I had a number of unanswered calls from Pedro Bessa. I had a feeling it might be something good. And, yes, I was right! He said that they could pay me €200 a month and I accepted it – although I thought the amount was still less than I deserved. But I was still very proud that for the first time in my life I was going to earn money for my scouting work. It was a huge step forward in my career, and I had no doubt that I was making progress! I was criticised by some people for accepting the job for so little money, but those people didn't understand the competition in this area or that I had a long way still to go before I made a name for myself. The other three scouts from the south area left, including the two who had won the internship. However, a new scout in my region, who had completed the same course as me in 2014, joined the club.

I started my second season on 13 September 2014, with a game between Sporting B and Portimonense at Alcochete. The demands on me had increased, and sometimes I had to watch two games in a weekend, which also involved producing two reports in my free time. My son was nine months old by then, and I remember it being physically and mentally demanding at the time. And I also had some other things to cope with on top of this; for example, in September I refused to go to a midweek game that would have meant me missing a day at my other job, and I hadn't had an easy time because my supervisor had been sacked after almost 15 years with the company. I had great ambitions in football and I wanted scouting to be my full-time job in the medium term, but I couldn't risk my full-time salary just yet.

On 2 October I went to see a game that would go down in history for Estoril Praia. They beat Panathinaikos from Greece 2-0 in the second round of the Europa League group stage, which was the club's first-ever victory in a game at this stage. The players I had recommended, Anderson Esiti and Kuca, played in the game, and both played well, which was remarkable. It made me proud that only months before they had been competing in the second tier.

So, what of my plans to go to America? I was still all set to go to Kansas City on 6 October. When I got in the taxi to take me to Lisbon airport, I was trying hard to hold back the tears. I was so nervous, and it took a lot of courage for me to leave my wife and son and fly to the other side of the world on my own. But I had to take the risk. I'm not proud of this, but I was still thinking about giving up on everything when I was in the boarding area! Although I was already

35 at the time, I still lacked maturity and confidence in many ways. But, somehow, I recovered my composure and got on the plane; I felt determined. The trip was quiet, the stopover in Philadelphia was fine and I arrived in Kansas City feeling much calmer. Waiting for me on arrival at the local airport was a driver holding a tablet with my name on it. I was reminded of my wife's words when we had arrived in London for my coaching course back in 2012 and had seen quite a few people waiting for others with their names written on papers or tablets: 'I hope one day you are important enough to have someone waiting for you with your name written on a board.' Well, only two years later, here I was. I couldn't say that I was important, but I had achieved it nonetheless. I went to the hotel in a limousine that the club had hired to pick me up, which made me think the USA really was as grand as I'd imagined. I'd already been to the USA in 2010, when I went to New York with my wife for a week. We saw the Statue of Liberty, the Empire State Building and went to a sporting event – the US tennis open. But now I wasn't in America for fun, it was with the clear goal of convincing those in charge of Sporting Kansas City that I could be helpful to the club.

The next day, Kerry picked me up at the hotel and drove me to the training centre. We had been exchanging messages for more than a year and it was great to finally get to know each other in person. I remember that I had a very clogged ear because of the previous day's flight, so my hearing wasn't the best, so our chat was not very fluent, but I remember him asking me about the Estoril/Panathinaikos game while we were at a coffee shop before we got to the training centre.

When we arrived, the first player I saw was right-back Chance Myers, who was recovering from a serious injury and had gone in for physiotherapy. I was introduced to coach Peter Vermes, the most important element in the whole structure. I don't remember being particularly nervous, but he was a figure who intimidated me, no doubt about it. We talked a bit about the 2014 World Cup, when the USA and Portugal had played each other, and then I went to watch a training session. I tried to pay attention to every detail of the session, always watching the better-known players like Graham Zusi – a bit of a perfectionist – or Benny Feilhaber, probably the best player in the team.

When the session was over, I went to Peter's office. Kerry was there too and I had a sort of interview. They asked me some tough but straightforward questions, such as, 'how would I structure a scouting department?' I don't think my answers were particularly good, although I wasn't tense, but I was not totally relaxed either. I was with two guys who were high-profile people and I was still feeling some jet lag – I was struggling to show them the best of me.

Afterwards, we went to lunch at an Italian restaurant and I remember talking about President Obama meeting the team a few weeks before in the White House, as a reward for them winning the MLS championship. I remember some of Peter's words very well, such as his view on the values and behaviours that everyone in a club should have: 'work ethic, intelligence and team first'. After lunch, there was one more training session, but this time with the young kids from the area. It was nice to see such great commitment from everybody. This first day had been incredible but very tiring, and I just wanted to go back to my hotel and have a rest.

The next day I watched another training session in the morning as the team were preparing for the match against Chicago Fire, and after lunch Kerry drove me to some of the club's other facilities. Somewhat unexpectedly, Kerry took me to the club president's office. Contrary to what I was expecting, Robb Heinemann seemed to be a simple man, dressed casually and with a completely down-to-earth demeanour.

During my free time, I explored the area near my hotel and I just had to taste the famous barbecue food from the city, which I can confirm is very good indeed. The hotel was excellent and it was such a good week for me, full of new experiences, like I was in another dimension.

Thursday, 9 October 2014

This was the day of the great game between Sporting Kansas City and Chicago Fire! I went to the stadium early with another guest, who was a friend of Peter's and an English coach. Kerry welcomed us and took us on a guided tour of the stadium, which had only been opened three years before and had been highly praised. I went on the pitch and in to the locker room and I took some photos for posterity.

The ceremony before the match was impressive: a chilling version of the American national anthem, followed by fireworks – all impeccably organised. When the game started I felt optimistic that Kansas would win, but after a penalty and another shot hitting the post I started to think that it could go wrong, which could be terrible for me, with my visit being associated with a poor result. I started to worry that it could mean the end for me as a potential future scout for the club! The game versus Chicago was also a decider to ensure qualification for the play-offs. Time was ticking by and I couldn't see a way that Kansas would score. But, thankfully, around the 80th minute, Graham Zusi's brilliant shot from outside the box went in! 1-0! Incredibly,

Chicago reacted quickly and created two clear opportunities, but some miraculous saves from the goalkeeper Andy Gruenebaum kept them at bay. Ironically, days before the match, in a conversation with Kerry I had told him that if I was to choose a best possible 11 from Estoril and Kansas players, i would choose this goalkeeper – who was voted man of the match in the game. Already in injury time, Dom Dwyer, the English striker, made it 2-0 with a good header! And the game was won! After the match, I went to the area where the players' families and coaches were waiting for them. It was the last time I was with Kerry and Peter before returning to Portugal, and I thanked Peter Vermes, and told him that I hoped we would keep in touch. He certainly told me that he would, which gave me a sense of mission accomplished.

I returned to Portugal hoping that I might have opened a door in Kansas, but my priority was to focus on Estoril and continue to do my best for them. Pedro was angry with me because I told him I had to travel abroad and would not be able to do any scouting at the games that weekend, so I had to compensate them for it. By the end of October, Pedro booked a meeting for us to analyse the work I'd done and outline my strategies. I had to be at my best and regain his trust. While I was waiting for him, I met coach José Couceiro, but only a 'good afternoon' was exchanged. Director Mário Branco appeared for part of the meeting, but there was no sign of an attempt from him to create a closer working relationship with me, even after the sensitive and personal email I had sent him when I had been 'fired' asking for advice. I admire Mário, and I think he is a winner and a very clever guy. He left Estoril and went to Hajduk Split in Croatia, and I still follow his career now. It would have been nice if he'd have worked a bit closer with me, but I still think he's a good person and I wish him all the best.

In November, I delivered a file of recommendations for the winter transfer market, in which I had selected what I thought were the best 11 of the second tier. I hoped my work would be used to make our team stronger in the near future. From the 11 players I had chosen, only two of them were not signed to a first-tier club in the subsequent two years. Fabrício was a particular stand-out choice that I am proud of from this report – although he wasn't signed by Estoril, he had a terrific season with Portimonense in 2017/18 in the first division, scoring 12 goals, and they then sold him to a Japanese team for €5 million.

Every weekend, come rain or shine, if I was sick or not, I never failed to get to any match again until the end of the season. I even made it to a game in the fourth tier, watching a team called Real Sport Clube, also known as Real Massamá. It was a team full of young talents – Nani was a product of their youth ranks. From this match, I highlighted winger Ença Fati and defender João Sousa, two players who were signed by a first-tier team (Moreirense) the following season. I think it's another pick that demonstrated my ability. At this point in my career, I was feeling pretty sure that my scouting skills were good enough to make a successful career in this area. My wife missed a bit of my support in Leonardo's first months, but she wasn't complaining anymore – I was living a tiring life that was very demanding, but I was managing to complete all my duties.

On top of my live games, Pedro would often send me games in other leagues to look at via Wyscout. By coincidence, he even asked me to assess a player from MLS, without knowing that I had watched a game for real there recently. From Colombia to Estonia, I would analyse any championship, always keeping a close eye on my favourite French second tier – I think there are some real scouting treasures in this league – players who could be cheap but very high quality – and even if Estoril didn't have the power to sign them, I thought this would be valuable knowledge for any club I might work for in the future.

As the January transfer window approached, like any ambitious and motivated scout, I was hoping that some signings would be made based on my work and ideas – but it didn't happen. Pedro and I really liked Bruno Santos, a right-back from a second-tier team, but no deal was done. However, Traffic managed to bring in a great quality Brazilian player, forward Leo Bonatini. But the biggest news for Estoril was that they decided to sell Kuca to a club in Turkey – Karabukspor. It was great business for the club as in six months they had sold a player that costed less than €200,000 for an amount near €1.6 million. It was good for my ego to see a player I had recommended, and who had come from the second division, develop so quickly. My confidence was high and I felt like I was a great asset for the club. This is what a good scout should do, recommend players who are not expensive but can generate a high profit in the future, not only in terms of performance on the field but also in terms of financial return.

That same month I was called to another meeting. Being a bit naive, I had some hope that the club were going to thank me because of the Kuca transfer. It's sort of funny now when I think back and see how wrong I was – they never even mentioned it, instead they were focussed on trying to find a replacement for him. In fantasy football I had a natural ability to succeed and make money consistently, but in the real world of football every euro I earned was very hard work – even when the club made a profit and I showed my competence. Once again, I had to carry on with a positive spirit and continue my journey.

The season was not going as well as the one before for Estoril. Coach José Couceiro wasn't keeping up with the level achieved in previous years, and in early March he was fired. The team hadn't reached the top half of the table and had already been eliminated from the Europa League – despite an epic match versus PSV Eindhoven ending in a 3-3 home draw – and the domestic cups. Rumours began to emerge that Traffic, the owners, wanted to sell the club to another investor. This meant instability and a very uncertain future for every one of us. So, in March 2015 I made the decision to start researching for possible new jobs, and I applied to all the clubs that I could think of that I thought would be a good next step in my career.

Around that time, I had to travel to Krakow in Poland to deliver some training as part of my day job, so I thought it would be a good idea to send some CVs to some Polish clubs in the hope I could get an interview there. I got two good responses, but most of my replies came from the USA, with several teams considering me as a possible option, in addition to Sporting Kansas City. I emailed Kerry to tell him that I wanted to leave Estoril and was trying to find a new club. I didn't feel that they were as interested in me as they had been before, and I thought that perhaps I hadn't made a good impression when I visited. I had also been a bit pushy afterwards, and I remember sending some over-the-top emails, including one in which I wrote that after some thought I had concluded that the trip to Kansas

City had made me more mature and more trusting of my communications skills and relationships with other people – but it was the truth. After having Peter and Kerry fire questions at me, I felt like I had become stronger; I was much more comfortable with the directors of my company with my improved communication skills, for example. Then I received an email from Kerry saying that they had hired a new scouting director, a Chilean named Jorge Alvial, who had worked for Chelsea for many years. He asked me if I could go to Madrid and meet him so he could evaluate me. It was great news and a light at the end of the tunnel. I took a few days off and enjoyed the fact that my in-laws had a house near the border with Spain. I stayed there one night and then I drove to Madrid.

On 21 April 2015, I was at a hotel in Madrid, face to face with Jorge Alvial. I made my presentation, and took my portfolio that I had put together, which now also included the work reports I had written for Estoril. Jorge told me about his career and the good relationships he'd had with the coaches at Chelsea, including José Mourinho and André Villas-Boas. After some time, he made me a proposal: Sporting Kansas City were interested in hiring me as a European scout and he told me how much they would be willing to pay me. Obviously, I told him I was interested and would be happy to work for the club. They were offering me more than double what Estoril were paying me, so it was progress at all levels. Me and Jorge talked about MLS and we both agreed that it was a league with enormous potential for growth and a good step forward in my career.

The next day, I went to watch a training session with the Getafe B team with Jorge because he wanted to see a player who Chelsea had signed in the past after his recommendation and they had become close friends. We also saw a training session with the Getafe first team, where he kept an eye on a young central defender who was impressing both of us, and he explained to me that when he had a feeling about a player he liked to act immediately, and he was fully confident in his instincts. It was an interesting and priceless experience for me to spend time with a man who was at the top in scouting terms – and had been for many years.

I returned to Portugal aware that I could have a future at SKC. A few days later, I received an email from Jorge confirming that he was going to recommend hiring me to Peter and Kerry. I thanked him for having confidence in me and confirmed that I was committed to Estoril until the end of May, but on 1 June I would be free to start.

I entered 'countdown' mode. I continued my scouting work and wrote my reports, but I had to prepare how I would tell Pedro that I was going to leave. When that day came, he reacted well and agreed that it was a wise decision due to the instability and uncertainty at the club. I finished this second season having watched 40 games and having produced all the related reports – a respectful number for a part-time scout. I even remember in one of my last games I drove around 200 miles to see a player and when I arrived there he was not in the squad, a complete nightmare for a scout! He had picked up an injury in one of the last training sessions of the week. Well, we have to live with these situations, it's part of the job.

The team finished the season in a disappointing 12th place after appointing a new coach, Fabiano Soares – a former Brazilian player who excelled at Compostela (Spain) at the peak of his career. In one of the final games of the season, Estoril lost 2-0 at Guimarães with two goals scored by Ricardo Valente, a player I had recommended at the end of the previous season. Guimarães also played João Afonso against Vitória, a defender I had recommended after watching him play in the third tier at the end of the previous season. They had both played an important part in the team's fifth-place finish. I can't say that if they had signed for Estoril we would have done better that season or that they would have performed well there, but they both succeeded where they went, and I think these recommendations in my reports go a long way to proving that I am a good scout and they help to build my reputation, which is based on real results. At the end of my employment with Estoril, I delivered my final work – shadow teams from the 2014/15 season. I reduced the number of players I proposed to 25 for each tier. Among the players I suggested from the second tier, I have to highlight Dalbert, a young Brazilian left-back who today plays for Inter Milan after they paid €20 million to sign him from Nice. Nice had also paid €2 million to sign him from Guimarães – who had once again done some good scouting in the second tier when they signed him from Académico Viseu.

So, I left Estoril with a clear conscience, knowing that I'd done a great job.

16

SPORTING KANSAS CITY
2015/16 (first season)

Monday, 1 June 2015

A new era was about to begin in my career! After two years working for Estoril, my third season as a scout was going to be with Sporting Kansas City! I felt really motivated but a bit nervous. I already knew how good a club they were, with a fantastic stadium and modern facilities. The club was set up in 1995 and is one of a small number of clubs that have played in every season in MLS since the beginning of the competition back in 1996. They had already won a few titles and the highlights were the 2000 and 2013 MLS titles. On the first day, I had a conference call with head coach Peter Vermes and Kerry Zavagnin, the assistant coach. Both won MLS as players in 2000 and formed the main coaching duo in 2013, so they are legends at the club. I was feeling really grateful for the opportunity. I was less nervous and much more involved than I had been in the interview I'd had at SKC the year before, but I was still not totally at ease with them.

In the middle of June, I decided to take a week off from my day job to watch football matches so I could make a strong start for my new club. I was asked to focus on

Portugal (first and second tier), Spain (second tier) and France (second tier) and I was told that the main gap we needed to fill in the upcoming transfer window was central defender – and I absolutely agreed. The platform that the club used to watch video clips was InStat. It was a little different to Wyscout, but still a really good tool.

After doing a lot of work watching video footage that first week in June, I started to recommend some central defenders. My first suggestions were the players I already knew from Portugal, such as the Brazilian Roberto Cunha, who in my opinion was being wasted in the Portuguese second division. I knew him from the work I'd done for Estoril and I thought he was the right fit for us if we were trying to go for an undervalued and cheap player of good quality. From the Spanish second tier, I recommended a few players who were coming to the end of their contracts so the timing was very good – Victor Laguardia from Alavés was the best of them. Instead of reporting to Jorge Alvial, I was asked to send the players I'd spotted to Kerry for him to analyse. He liked Laguardia a lot and, along with Roberto, they were listed as possibles. It was a good start for me.

The first few weeks at the club were intense. On top of this pressure, it had been a difficult period in my full-time job as there had been a number of changes amongst the staff I was working with, which had meant constantly adapting to new roles according to the company's needs. However, I was able to manage these changes as well as the demands from my football job, so I was happy that I coped OK.

30 July 2015

My first official scouting match for SKC was Belenenses vs IFK Gothenburg in a Europa League qualifying round, and the star of that game was Carlos Martins who scored two goals in a 2-1 win at Belém. Carlos had an interesting profile and possibly was the right fit for MLS, but he was already 33 and SKC had a peculiar policy of not hiring foreign players over 30, which limited my options, although it was a policy that I fully backed. In August, the championships started in Portugal and I started my fieldwork with enthusiasm.

However, the MLS transfer window was near to closing and my first big disappointment was just around the corner: the only foreign player that SKC signed was Jordi Quintillà, a former Barcelona B player who was a free agent after failing at AC Ajaccio – a French second-tier club that I used to follow. I didn't have a high opinion of him – he was a good passer with fine technique, but he was unable to make well-timed vertical passes and was very soft in challenges. Just because a player has Barcelona on his CV, it doesn't mean he is good. This can be a tricky situation for a scout, and I try not to be swayed by the clubs a player has played for. It's often good when a player has had youth-level experience at a team like Barcelona, Ajax or Juventus, but it doesn't necessarily mean they are a great player. The other signing was Amobi Okugo, a versatile player with a lot of MLS experience, who could play in a number of positions, including central defender. This was not what I had expected, and I think there were better options that had not been taken.

At that time, I remember dreaming I was in the SKC stadium and our electronic scoreboard had a picture of Laguardia on it, announcing him in our starting 11. I was totally convinced that he would fit perfectly into our team, with the warrior profile that he had, and there was no transfer fee as his contract was ending. In the real world,

Kerry told me that Laguardia's agent had actually been 'stubborn' and there was no chance of an agreement, with the player renewing his contract with Alavés a few days later.

The team performed really well in the US Open Cup, the American equivalent of a national cup, with a trio of players playing particularly well: Benny Feilhaber, an attacking midfielder, Kristian Nemeth, a Hungarian striker playing as a winger (he failed at Liverpool when he was younger but was a key player for SKC) who could easily escape in midfield and score great goals, and Dom Dwyer, our English centre-forward and a prolific goalscorer. We reached the final of the Open Cup, which was due to be played on 30 September, but in the league the team went into a real negative spiral just after the transfer window closed. A terrible 5-0 home defeat against San Jose Earthquakes began a run of eight games with just one win. I always try to watch the games live, even when they are on very late, which is quite often because Portugal is six hours ahead of Kansas City, and I remember staying awake around that time to watch an away game against Columbus Crew. With ten minutes to go we were winning 2-1, but we ended up losing 3-2; it was frustrating, especially as I was fighting to keep my eyes open to watch it and my reward was another cruel defeat. I also haven't forgotten the time when I woke up in the middle of the night, at about 4.30 in the morning, to check the score in our game against Portland. I turned the computer on and it was 0-0, but after a few minutes I saw Nemeth dribbling past almost the entire Timbers team and shooting the ball into the back of the net! I thought I was dreaming, it was such a fantastic goal. We ended up winning the game 1-0, and the goal was one of the best in MLS that year.

30 September 2015

The big night finally arrived, the final of the US Open Cup. Our opposition were Philadelphia Union, who had been drawn to play at home. They were not one of the better teams in the league, but it was expected to be an even match. I booked leave the day after so I could watch the game live without the pressure of having to go to work early the next day. It was a great moment for me because for the first time in my career the club I was working for were in a cup final. The game wasn't exactly exciting. Philadelphia scored first and were the slightly better team, but in the second half Nemeth's skill levelled the game after a pass from Zusi found his right foot and he put the ball in the net. It finished 1-1 so the winner would be decided on penalties. Our great goalkeeper Tim Melia was once again brilliant, making two decisive saves, leaving Quintillà to take the penalty for the match. He scored and we won the cup! Although I had only started working for SKC four months before, I felt a strong connection with the team, and seeing them lift the cup was a fantastic experience. Being part of history is something money can't buy – it's priceless! I will always be able to say that when SKC won the US Open Cup I was working for them as a scout. Nothing can take that away from me. And it was just the beginning for me, I wanted to see so many more wins.

Days before the match, I had had another moment of great personal fulfilment. Every week I chose which games I would watch, and I always tried to see teams from Northern Portugal or the Islands when they came to play around Lisbon. In the last weekend of September, one of the games I decided to go to was Benfica vs Paços Ferreira. It was the first time I'd been to the Stadium of Light for work, and I can't deny that throughout my childhood and teenage years it was probably the place that I loved the most in the whole world. When I was choosing my profession, I never thought that one day I would get paid to come here and watch Benfica play! Life can be difficult sometimes, and we often feel like we are being punished when we're in situations that are unfair, but this was the opposite: life had given me this great experience. I had to watch the game but still behave professionally and not forget that I was there representing another club. Benfica won 3-0, and I tried not to move when the goals were scored, but the Benfica supporter next to me hugged me after the second and third goals so I thought it would be OK if I celebrated with him.

In the middle of this frantic beginning at SKC, there was dramatic news at the club – Jorge Alvial would be leaving the club at the end of the season. I was really disappointed because it would have been such a great experience to work with a man of his profile. I never found out exactly what happened, but I think there may have been a difference of opinion among the staff. Jorge went on to work for Atlanta, a new MLS team, and nowadays he is the scouting director at new MLS team Cincinnati FC, after he worked at Manchester United with José Mourinho, with whom he has worked before when he was at Chelsea.

The MLS regular season finishes at the end of October, and then it's time for the play-offs. We qualified in sixth place in the Western Conference, the last position that guarantees a place in the play-offs, but we would have to play our game away against the Portland Timbers. To be honest, I didn't feel much confidence in the team, mainly because of the central defender issue. Our full-backs didn't inspire much confidence either, but we had a strong core with Tim Melia, an excellent goalkeeper, Matt Besler, one of the league's best defenders, Sony Mustivar, a defensive midfielder who was not great but could recover the ball well, the reliable midfielder Paulo Nagamura, who was doing a great job replacing the injured ex-Wigan player Roger Espinoza, and Benny Feilhaber, a very good player who could connect with the talented attacking trio of Zusi, Nemeth and Dwyer. We always played 4-3-3, whether the game was at home or away, but sometimes the midfield triangle could switch to a more defensive double pivot. We went to Portland to win, and the game was broadcast on Eurosport. I recorded the game so I could watch it early the next morning, without finding out the result, but I didn't tell my wife what I had planned to do, so when I woke she said something like, 'I saw on the internet that Kansas lost, and even the goalkeepers scored goals.' I didn't take much notice as I thought she was joking – it didn't seem likely that the goalkeepers would have scored, as any football follower knows. So, I watched the recording. Portland scored first in the second half, but we managed to equalise through Ellis's goal three minutes from time. A magnificent Nemeth goal put us ahead in extra time, but two minutes from the end it was Portland's turn for a late equaliser after some poor defending. The decision again went to penalties, as seemed to be a tradition in the club's recent history, having won the championship in 2013 and the cup in 2012 and 2015 the same way. But this time we didn't get a happy ending. I wouldn't say that penalties are more about luck, but we lost by a millimetre, with one of the failed penalties hitting two posts. After 11 sets of penalties, Portland took the lead when their goalkeeper scored his penalty and our usual substitute goalkeeper, young Kempin who came in to replace the injured Melia, failed with his shot. This difficult elimination was hard to take, but at least I now understood what Patricia was saying! That game ended the season for us, which could still be considered a good one after winning the cup and losing in such a close tie in the play-offs.

It was now time to start work on the next season. I felt that signing a central defender was the number-one priority, and I was already well aware of the options that had arisen in the markets I was following. My favourite, because of the value he could add versus the amount he would cost, was Roberto Cunha, who was playing in the third division in Portugal for Loures. Coincidentally, his team had been drawn against Boavista from the first division in a Portuguese Cup knock-out competition, which was excellent for me as it meant I could see how he performed against a top-level team. I invited the agent Paulo Teixeira to come with me, who I'd been introduced to by Kerry when I started working for SKC. The game was good, with Boavista winning 2-1, but only in extra time. Roberto had a very successful game and the next day he was awarded 'man of the match' by *Record*, one of the big newspapers in Portugal. Paulo was amazed by Roberto and praised me for my work. Two weeks after we'd been eliminated from the play-offs, Kerry made a trip to Portugal to watch some games with me, including one in which Roberto was playing. I thought it was amazing how quickly Kerry had reacted after such a tough defeat to switch focus and start thinking and planning for the next season. This is a champion mentality.

At this time, my life away from scouting was also under control. Leonardo was growing well and was happy, and Patricia had taken a year off from her job because we thought it was the right decision for all of us. I would be able to spend more time on my scouting tasks and keep on top of my finance work. The extra money I was earning from scouting didn't cover Patricia's salary, but it was still the right decision because it kept our family life stable and allowed me to give my scouting career my best shot.

6 November 2015

I booked half a day's leave to meet Kerry in the afternoon and go to Estoril vs Académica with him at night. His trip had been carefully planned, with a schedule that included games, meetings with players, agents, and a potential coach for our B team. And, of course, he had some work to do with me watching videos, so that I could show him the players from my shadow teams from the five leagues I was covering. In that first game, the focus was on Gerso, an Estoril winger who was having an excellent season and a player who I strongly backed as a future signing for SKC. The game went well for him, and Kerry liked his profile – his Portugal visit got off to a good start. The next day we did some work in his hotel, watching games and analysing wingers that I had picked in my shadow teams. From memory, I think we watched players like Gerso and Kuca in more detail. Kuca was the player who I had suggested to Estoril and was now at Belenenses, on loan from his Turkish club because of problems he'd had adapting to the country. We also watched players I'd picked out from the Belgian league, such as Edmilson (playing for St. Truiden, now at Standard de Liege), and the French Ligue 2, such as Opa N'Guette (playing for Valenciennes, now at Metz). After sending my files to Kerry on Saturday, he also looked at the defensive midfielders and central defenders I'd recommended and was pleased with what he saw, praising my work. Over the next few days, he got to see some of them in live matches, and I was anxious to see if they would live up to the expectations I had created.

On the Sunday we went to see Roberto Cunha, the central defender playing for Loures, who was going to play in the Sintrense Field. The pressure was on because the impression the player made on Kerry would be fundamental in whether or not he was signed. For me, a good scout should be able to discover players who are playing at a lower competitive level and know that he can perform well at a higher level, and this was what I thought of Roberto; I saw him as the perfect example of an undervalued and financially accessible player who could be competent at a higher level. The Portuguese third division has many talented players year after year who could be signed for higher division clubs and go on to perform well. But the lower league games are almost always played in near-empty stadiums with old infrastructures. The games are not always very good quality, and a scout has to focus to find the players that stand out. That afternoon in Sintra, that's exactly what happened: the seats were almost empty, the play was poor quality and Roberto did well but wasn't outstanding because of the way the game was played. Although his team won 1-0, not even the best defenders in the world, like Chiellini or Varane, would have been noticed in this game.

Roberto was ruled out after Kerry said he didn't feel there was anything special about him. All I could do was accept his decision and continue my work. It's hard for me to hide my frustration sometimes, but it's something I've got better at since I started coaching, which I think is an important thing to learn for any scout.

The next day, agent Paulo Teixeira called a meeting between us and the marketing and IT managers of Sport Lisboa e Benfica at the club. The aim was to talk a little about the software products that SKC had and the products other companies had to offer. After the meeting, we were offered a guided tour of the stadium, and for me it was fascinating to be part of something like this, even more so because it was at the club I supported. Ironically, I only received this sort of VIP treatment in my home country by working with a foreign club.

That night, we went to watch Belenenses vs Tondela – there were players that I had recommended in both teams. It was an interesting game, and Tondela's defensive midfielder Lucas Souza, who I had suggested in my shadow team, had a good game. Although the winger Kuca did not convince Kerry of his worth, he liked Lucas and both right-backs, André Geraldes (Belenenses) and Edu Machado (Tondela), who were also in my shadow teams.

To be honest, this early work that I did was far from refined. Some of the things I did didn't make much sense, like having five players from the same league in some positions. I should have filtered them a bit more and decided which were the best two. At the time I also didn't know how much SKC had to spend on players, which could explain some of my dubious choices. I wanted to point out players who I thought were good, but I didn't want to include players who I didn't think would make the move to MLS, so I didn't include players from the top teams. Instead I tried to look for promising young players who were playing for smaller teams, such as Naranjo (Nastic Tarragona) from Spain's second division. Looking back at the players I suggested at the beginning of November 2015,

Sergio Leon was one of the best as he is now the number-one striker in the Spanish second tier – at the time he was an Elche player, but today he is established at Betis Seville, a good Spanish league team, and he is valued at around €5 million at the age of 29.

Kerry made a second trip to Portugal in December, and we went to see Estoril against the Madeira team Nacional to watch Gerso one more time. His performance was not as good as in the previous match, but still good enough to show his talent. In that game, I was embarrassed by Yohan Tavares's poor performance, an Estoril central defender who I had recommended and knew well. He was unrecognisable and continued to play poorly after that, so I had to remove him from my list and he never got back on to it. It's one of those times in my career when I feel like I failed, and it serves to remind me to always reflect on my decisions: I knew the player well, I knew he had value and had been playing consistently well over the last three seasons, but suddenly his performance level dropped and he couldn't recover, and he had no excuses like an injury or age. I couldn't necessarily have predicted it, but I felt like my intuition had let me down.

Kerry continued his trip in Northern Portugal with Marc dos Santos, a Portuguese-Canadian who had now agreed to be the new coach of our B team, who were called Swope Park Rangers. I left for Porto the following Friday to join them and went to see Boavista vs Estoril, which was another milestone in my career, because for the first time I was scouting in Porto at the Stadium of Bessa, one of the most emblematic in Portugal.

The next day, while I was driving Kerry to a match, I talked to him about some interesting players who could be good options for us. The number-one player I mentioned was Diego Rubio, a young centre-forward from Sporting who couldn't find a place in the first team and was on loan to Valladolid in the Spanish second division, but who was still rarely playing. I knew Rubio well, particularly from a series of games I had watched at Sporting B the previous season when I was still scouting for Estoril. He scored a lot of goals there and showed enough quality that I was convinced.

That night we went to Paços de Ferreira where we saw an historic 6-0 rout – Paços beating União da Madeira. I had a couple of possible players in both teams, and Kerry was very impressed with Andrezinho and the now famous and successful Wolverhampton Wanderers player Diogo Jota. I had both these players on my list, but because they were so young I didn't see them as realistic options, as they were likely to have other, more attractive, options than MLS. I met Marc dos Santos at that game, and, as soon as I started talking to him, I felt he had a very positive energy and lots of charisma. I also knew he had an excellent sense of humour and a great passion for football as I got to know him a little better during our marathon football weekend. The next day, the three of us went to see three more matches, from morning to night, in three different regions of the country. The day was very intense and unforgettable. The match we were most excited to see was the last game, Tondela vs Braga, where heavy rain was waiting for us. We went there to see 'my' Lucas Souza, the Tondela midfielder, who was simply the 'man of the match'. Playing on form like this, he was certainly good enough to play in MLS. I thought I had scored myself some points after this game.

In the following two months, I closely followed the club's moves in the market. Two experienced players were hired for the wing, Brad Davis and Justin Mapp, but I didn't think they'd bring what we needed. They were free agents, but both were already past their best. This is another potentially tricky situation for a scout: sometimes a player who appears to be cheap can turn out to be very expensive! A free agent doesn't always mean a great deal.

They also confirmed the signing of Lawrence Olum, who I wasn't a fan of, and Nuno André Coelho, whose physical problems and recent lack of fitness was a bit of a concern. The announcement that the team were signing a Portuguese defender led some friends to call and congratulate me, including fellow scouts from other clubs, but I was a little embarrassed because I hadn't recommended the player, although having a Portuguese player in the squad was good for me because it meant the press would start to follow SKC more closely.

I also thought strengthening the defensive wings should have been a priority – the best player we had was Canadian Marcel de Jong, but he ended up leaving. There are salary cap rules in MLS so I don't know if that played a part in the decisions, but I thought we needed some better players in these positions than we had at the time. We also lost one of our best players, Nemeth, who was transferred to a team in Qatar, and we needed to reinforce the midfield properly. Lucas Souza, who was coming to the end of his contract with Tondela, had been my best pick. Although I didn't necessarily agree with their choices, the decision makers had a lot more experience than me in MLS and had achieved good results in the recent past.

We kept our core team of Melia, Besler, Zusi, Espinoza, Feilhaber, Dwyer, and our coaching staff did a great job with some of these players. Melia was a goalkeeper who had been unable to secure a place in the teams he'd played for, but he found his confidence with SKC and became one of the best in the league; Besler and Zusi were two USA internationals who were key players; Espinoza was an Honduras international player with Premier League experience who returned to SKC the year before; Feilhaber had been a bit unstable before coming to SKC, but had his best years with the club; and Dwyer, an English player from the 2012 Combine Draft (a yearly event when teams choose the best players from colleges), was a productive striker with great energy.

I found it difficult to accept the signing decisions, but in January 2016 it was announced that a new director would be joining the club – Brian Bliss, a former US international who spent most of his career in Germany in the second division. I had known his name since 1990 because of my Italian World Cup stickers, and I had a feeling that I would get along very well with him. He would be supervising my work from now on, so I felt more positive.

All the players from my scouting work had been ignored, but, just when I was losing all hope, two opportunities presented themselves. I was told to concentrate on young strikers and I again mentioned Diego Rubio as one of the best options.

Around that time I received an email from Kerry with a list of players that agents had offered to the club, and on it was 'Diego Rubio Kostner'. Days later an agreement was reached between Sporting and Valladolid and the player arrived on loan for six months, but with an option to buy. He was going to be a back-up for Dom Dwyer, our number-one striker. This was a real achievement for me – there was a player on the team sheet who had been recommended by me! Reviewing my notes from back then, I described Rubio to Kerry as follows:

> He played for Sporting B between January/ May 2015, and I followed him closely because I used to watch Sporting B when I was scouting in the second tier for Estoril. He did very well during that period. I thought he would make the Sporting A squad that season, but he was dropped and went to Valladolid. The experiences that he already had in his career and his maturity level for 22 years old, makes him a good option for us. He works a lot, can score great goals from outside the area (I saw one really good one against Viseu), and he is often in the right place to score. When his trust levels are high, he is prolific. Probably needs some restoration after not playing much at Valladolid, but he is a player who could score 15 goals in MLS.

There was also a possibility that we would sign Kevin Oliveira, who was playing in Sporting da Covilhã in the Portuguese second division, on loan from Benfica. I had included him in my shadow team, and both Kerry and Marc dos Santos liked the player, seeing him as a strong possibility to be part of our B team and in the future move into the first team. With the excellent help of agent Paulo Teixeira – who had a strong relationship with the club – an agreement was reached! Kevin moved to Kansas City to play for the B team. Almost in stoppage time, I scored my two goals!

When the season started, I was more nervous now I had some players in the squad, but we won the first game 1-0 against Seattle with a goal from Nuno André Coelho. In the first five games we got four wins! Nuno played in every game, and he played well, so my first impressions were that I'd been wrong in my assessment. I'm not stubborn about my opinions, and if I'm wrong, I'm happy to admit it. There is a famous Portuguese quote that goes: 'only an intelligent man can change his opinion, the dumbest one never will.'

In April, I met Brian Bliss face to face when he came to Portugal to watch some matches with me and follow Erik Palmer-Brown, our player who had been sent on loan to FC Porto B for a year. I liked him a lot. He was very different to Jorge Alvial, but I was very confident I'd settle well with him. We were starting to work on the attacking midfielder and winger options for the summer transfer window.

In May, at the end of my first season, I delivered my updated shadow teams, and I had decided to do an extra report, which I thought was particularly important as it was a list of my suggestions of the best players who were coming to the end of their contracts in the leagues I was covering, mostly in the Spanish second tier. There were a lot of good players who could be signed on a free transfer. I had watched a total of 74 live matches, which was an impressive number. I wouldn't have been able to watch this many if Patricia hadn't put her career on hold. I don't think my family life was affected by it, but mainly because of her. The only bad thing I remember was suffering from tonsillitis for the first time, which I think was related to attending some matches at night in cold weather. In one season for SKC I had seen the same number of matches as I had done in two seasons with Estoril. I had more freedom to choose the matches I saw with SKC and I didn't have to produce reports about every game, which allowed me to manage my time in a different and more efficient way. My notes – and my memory – helped me to give my opinion about a player in a quick and efficient manner when asked, and I could set my own deadlines for delivering my work. I was happier with this way of working, and I was optimistic about my future with SKC. The first 12 months had been pretty good and I was developing good relationships with the people I was working with.

My first big win in England— 'You The Manager' August 2007 Manager of the Month! The Daily Mirror requested a photo to be printed in the newspaper and my mother took this nice photo of me at the Palace of Queluz. I had much more hair back then!

Finally I made it and I was 'You The Manager' champion 2009/10! This is the winning photo and I could finally savour the taste of the champagne. My dream came true! Patrícia, my wife, took this photo in our living room.

After a scouting department meeting, this photo was taken at Estoril Praia headquarters — my first team that will always be special in my life. The two seasons I spent there was a great start for my career.

With Gerso Fernandes in the locker room at SKC stadium after winning the cup in 2017.

With Nuno André Coelho, a Portuguese player signed by SKC before the 2016 season.

The first time I went to Kansas City, it was amazing to be invited by SKC assistant coach, Kerry Zavagnin, to see the club and the fantastic stadium. I was still working at Estoril but a future move to SKC was my goal.

My sweetest moment so far, at SKC, holding a trophy after winning the US Open Cup 2017 against the NY Red Bulls. These are the kind of things that money can't buy. And these are the greatest rewards from our work – raising cups!

January 2013 – Bild newspaper page mentioning my Winter Champion achievement! My first big win in Germany and a Suzuki Swift as a prize! In the end I changed the car for money and it was the right decision. The best was yet to come.

My squad that won the Bild Super-Manager crown! I did an excellent job selecting this group of players but some comments from other competitors on the social networks were that the squad was nothing special. I had a laugh reading that. I enjoyed the most spectacular and best win of my Fantasy Football career!

200th match for SKC – ending my third season with SKC at the Portuguese Cup Final 2018! By coincidence it was my 200th match and a milestone in my career. In the end Aves won against Sporting for one of the biggest surprises ever.

Schweinsteiger scores against Portugal in the 2006 World Cup to help me reach my first podium finish in an international Fantasy Football competition.

Frank Lampard – the man that every fantasy team had to have in my best years! I couldn't build a team without him!

Darren Bent at Sunderland was a cheaper striker but he helped me to win a monthly and the yearly prize back in 2009/10.

Gareth Bale scores against Arsenal in 2010. That goal started my final run to the 'You The Manager' win.

Steven Gerrard scored a brace versus Burnley in 2010 to give me a big lead that I kept until the end to win the 'You The Manager' title.

Alex Meier from Eintracht Frankfurt and Jerome Boateng from Bayern Munich, two important pieces in my winning team.

Borussia Dortmund's Polish duo of Lewandowski and Blaszczykowski were decisive in my Bild *win.*

Anderson Esiti and Kuca (right) playing Europa League vs PSV Eindhoven. Estoril signed these two players on my recommendation – a few months before this match both were playing Second Division football.

Diego Rubio – a fantastic 2018 season with a ratio of 0.92 goals per game put him on a par with MLS stars like Zlatan Ibrahimovic and Josef Martinez.

Diego Rubio arguing with Ashley Cole from LA Galaxy – my present as a scout crossing with my FF past.

MLS Open Cup Final 2017 – Kevin Oliveira comes on in place of Diego Rubio. Both players were recommended by me and won the trophy for Sporting Kansas City against the New York Red Bulls.

Gerso Fernandes, a great success in MLS. One of the best professionals I met, a fantastic example of life inspiration and how to overcome adversity. I will always be grateful to him.

Yohan Croizet dedicates a goal to his late mother with Johnny Russell coming to congratulate him.

Diego Rubio and Gerso celebrating a goal for Sporting Kansas City in front of a celebrating crowd.

▲ SUITED TO THE JOB Grant must revive West Ham's fortunes

'AMMERS AV THEIR MAN

By DARREN LEWIS

AVRAM GRANT is expected to be appointed as West Ham's new boss today.

The Israeli will confirm one of the biggest open secrets in the Premier League when he pens a four-year deal to become Gianfranco Zola's successor at Upton Park.

And his first task will be to persuade disillusioned skipper Scott Parker (below) his future lies at the club.

Co-owners David Gold and David Sullivan insist the midfielder is the only player they will not listen to offers for. But a number of clubs, including Liverpool, are said to be keen on Parker, who is despondent after being cut from Fabio Capello's World Cup squad without playing a single minute of England's two warm-up games.

Gold said yesterday: "After an hour (of meeting Grant), we knew we could work with this manager. We are very optimistic.

"It's time for the football club to get some stability with people that have been there, done that and got the T-shirt. The relationship between the manager and the chairman is critical.

"In our case it's two chairmen so it's even more difficult."

Grant will be tasked with ensuring there is no repeat of the relegation threat which

made for such a dramatic campaign at the Hammers.

Gold added: "We can't put our fans through that again. We want to put together a team that is better than last year. We were very fortunate. Normally 35 points gets you relegated.

"What we need is a manager who has achieved, has experience. We are not in a position where we can take on young, inexperienced managers."

A statement on the Hammers website said last night: "West Ham will make a formal announcement of the club's new manager within 24 hours.

"The club have been conducting a thorough recruitment programme and made excellent progress.

"The squad are set to report back for pre-season training on July 5, meaning the new manager will have plenty of time to put together his squad."

Portugal winger Luis Boa Morte has been offered a new deal in a shock U-turn by the club. He returned in April after nine months out with a serious knee injury.

But he had looked to be on the way out after criticising the co-owners' in a TV interview. But Grant has requested he be kept on.

The club are releasing strikers Ilan and Mido.

RESULTS & FIXTURES

FOOTBALL
INTERNATIONAL FRIENDLIES
Albania.............(1) 1 Andorra......(0) 1
Salihi 44
Azerbaijan.....(0) 0 Honduras...(0) 0
Belarus.............(0) 0 Sweden......(0) 1
Wilhelmsson 48
Greece...............(0) 0 Paraguay....(2) 2
Vera 9
Barrios 25
Norway.............(0) 0 Ukraine......(1) 1
Zozulya 78
Poland..............(0) 0 Macedonia..(2) 1
Sikov 28
Romania...........(0) 0 Macedonia...(3) 1
Sikov 28
Zimbabwe........(0) 0 Brazil............(2) 3
Nilmar 33
Michel Bastos 42
Robinho 44
Elano 56

CRICKET
FRIENDS PROVIDENT T20
Grace Road: Derbyshire 165-5 beat Leicestershire 154-8 (McDonald 67) by 11 runs.

TENNIS
FRENCH OPEN
Men's singles quarter-finals: 2 R Nadal (Spa) bt 19 N Almagro 7-6 (7-2) 7-6 (7-3) 6-4; 22 J Melzer (Aut) bt 3 N Djokovic (Ser) 3-6 2-6 6-2 7-6 (7-3) 6-4.

Women's singles quarter-finals: 4 J Jankovic (Ser) bt Y Shvedova (Kaz) 7-5 6-4; 7 S Stosur (Aus) bt 1 S Williams (US) 6-2 6-7 (2-7) 8-6. Women's doubles semi-finals: 1 S Williams (USA) & V Williams (USA) bt 3 L Huber (USA) & A Medina Garrigues (Spa) 2-6 6-2 6-4; 12 K Peschke (Cze) & K Srebotnik (Slo) bt 2 N Llagostera Vives & NJ Martinez Sanchez (Spa) 3-6 6-4 6-4.

Mixed doubles semi-finals: Y Shvedova (Kaz) & J Knowle (Aut) bt V King (USA) & C Kas (Ger) 6-4 6-4; K Srebotnik (Slo) & N Zimonjic (Ser) bt 3 N Llagostera Vives (Spa) & O Marach (Aut) 4-6 3-9 9.

Boy's Singles 3rd rd: 11 R Olivo (Arg) bt A Hewitt (Gbr) 6-4 7-6 (7-3).

TODAY'S FOOTBALL
INTERNATIONAL FRIENDLIES
Germany v S Herzegovina (7.30pm)
Italy v Mexico (6.15pm)
Spain v South Korea (5pm)
TODAY'S CRICKET
INT'L TRIANGULAR SERIES
Hampshire v Kent (7pm)
Middlesex v Sussex (6.15pm)
Warks v Northants (5.30pm)
Yorkshire v Derbyshire (5.30pm)

I was invited to promote the World Cup game and it was great to be a part of it. Sharing a newspaper page with Cristiano Ronaldo doesn't happen every day!

Giving an interview to one of the biggest newspapers in the world was an amazing achievement for me. I felt really proud and honoured.

17

SPORTING KANSAS CITY
2016/2017 (second season)

July 2016

My second season at Sporting Kansas City started in the aftermath of Euro 2016, which Portugal won. I don't think it was our best national team performance, but we had Cristiano Ronaldo and he was the deciding factor – not only because of his goals and assists but also because he made us have a winner's mentality, which is sometimes the biggest hurdle to overcome. He made us believe we could do it and the Portuguese people had their well-deserved party – finally!

I watched the match at home with my in-laws and, of course, Patricia and Leonardo – who fell asleep on the floor during the match – he must have been dreaming about the best moment in Portugal's football history! I was so happy and I thought this win compensated for some of the disappointment of previous great teams that had lost in semi-finals; in particular, our Euro 84 and Euro 2000 losses against France, both in extra time and both a bit unfair. The next day I had to work, but me and my colleagues found time to watch the winners' parade across Lisbon that was live on TV.

I followed the tournament closely but at the same time started work on videos in two new leagues that I decided to cover for SKC: Norway and Sweden. The seasons for these two Scandinavian countries are played at the same time of year as the USA, from March to December. I didn't have extensive knowledge of these two leagues, but I realised that there were lots of transfers from these leagues to the MLS and vice-versa. So, I thought that maybe I could come up with some good options. Some players' contracts would end in December, so they would be available at the right time for MLS, when our major transfer window opens, so it made sense to become an expert in these leagues. My next shadow team deadline was around November 2016, so I had enough time to put together a very good team from these leagues.

The only transfers for SKC in the summer window were two young players who were already USA/Canada based: Cameron Porter and Emmanuel Appiah. Once again, I was disappointed as I hadn't contributed to improving the squad, and I wasn't sure about these two players. However, I was happy with some decisions; for example, Jordi Quintillà was waived and Amadou Dia was traded. I was happy to see a young Colombia player, Jimmy Medranda, having more playing time at left-back, and despite it not being his best position he still showed that he could play. It was also starting to look likely that Kevin Oliveira would be promoted to the first team as he was playing so well! He was scoring and assisting well for Swope Park Rangers, who competed at USL, a sort of second division in the USA/ Canadian soccer world. But then, sadly, I got a message from Kevin's agent saying, 'Kevin broke his knee'. At first, I thought it was a joke, but at the same time I thought Paulo Teixeira wouldn't joke about this kind of stuff. The season was over for Kevin Oliveira, and his dream of being promoted to the first team was delayed indefinitely. This was a huge blow to me too.

The team's results at this time were pretty average; we were chasing play-off qualification but always with ups and downs. Nuno André Coelho started strongly but he had some muscular problems and he was now more out of the team than in it. Diego Rubio was having much less game time than I thought too, even though he was supposed to be Dom Dwyer's back-up. However, when called, Rubio answered well with a good goal in a cup match which was also his first MLS goal. But our best player was still Dwyer, even though he was not having his best season.

In August I started going to live games and was also preparing for a trip to Kansas City in September. I had agreed to go once a year to watch some of the games and training sessions. It was important for me to go there so I could see things live that you can't always see in video. This is part of the 'art of scouting': you can evaluate a player on video, but seeing a player live gives you a much more accurate picture and you are much less likely to make an error in judgement. I chose the dates to go so I could see an MLS match vs Houston Dynamo and a CONCACAF Champions League (CCL) match against Vancouver Whitecaps. As a bonus, Swope Park Rangers were also playing at home that weekend against Tulsa Roughnecks in the USL.

This time it was much easier for me to leave my family and my emotions were much more under control. My managers from my day job were great and allowed me to go without any issues. I was excited and wanted to show more confidence than I had done two years before. When I arrived I had a very nice welcome from everybody. Because of our Portuguese connection and of course speaking the same language, it was great to have the SPR coaching duo of Marc dos Santos and Nikola Popovic there, and they were so kind to me, taking me out to dinner and showing me lots of interesting things in the city that I hadn't seen on my first visit. I spent most of my time with Brian, showing him the players that I had been following. The winger position was a priority at that time, and I clearly remember watching seven or eight wingers on video and ranking them. We had four or five players in the squad who could be played as wingers, but we really needed a big improvement.

Gameday: Sporting Kansas City vs Houston Dynamo

I could feel the pressure. We were playing against a team who were having a terrible season, but it was a must-win match. We started very strong and took a two-goal lead before the first half an hour, with a magnificent goal from Roger Espinoza and another from Jacob Petersen. But then our midfield lost control of the game and Houston started to dominate the match. Amazingly, they scored twice and when we reached the last quarter of the game it was 2-2. By this time Nuno had already left the match with an injury and Diego Rubio was benched without hope of coming on. Then our super striker Dwyer made it 3-2 with his killer instinct, but in injury time, after a silly foul in midfield, we conceded a free kick and Houston scored an equaliser. Final result – 3-3! This time I experienced the tense environment with the other staff members after the game. Some people were a bit down, but thankfully it wasn't as bad as I thought it would be.

The next day I went to see SPR vs Tulsa and we won easily, 3-0. I was impressed with some of our players, namely Tyler Pasher, Kris Tyrpak and Dane Kelly – three guys on the attacking line. It was a great game to watch, and I thought that our team was much stronger than the opposition. Marc dos Santos was doing a brilliant job; I'm just a player scout, but I thought he could be a top-team coach in Europe one day. I also saw Kevin Oliveira while I was there and we exchanged a few words; he looked a bit down as he was trying to recover his fitness and I tried to give him some words of comfort.

As part of my trip, a big meeting had been planned with all the people directly involved in the team to discuss the 2017 squad, which was the highlight of my trip. The meeting included Peter, Kerry, Zoran Savic – the Serbian assistant coach – Brian Bliss, Mike Jacobs – the assistant technical director, Ashley Wallace – performance analyst – and of course me! I was so proud to be in such an important meeting. We discussed each player and everybody was invited to give an opinion if there wasn't a consensus. I was feeling confident and brave enough to express some of my opinions even though they were against the general feeling. I thought we were going in the right direction though, and I agreed with most of the comments that were made. Afterwards I remember thinking that I would pay a huge amount of money to be at such an important meeting in a professional club, and I was so lucky to be there!

I still had another match to go to – CCL against Vancouver – but it was not a priority for the season. As we were struggling in the league and CCL had a strange fixture list – because the knock-out phase was played in the next season – we decided to play our less-used players in the game, so at least I would see Diego Rubio playing from the beginning! It was an unforgettable night because of the thunderstorm and lightning that suspended the match for more than an hour. The game was pretty average, but I was impressed by Alphonso Davies, a 15-year-old kid from Vancouver (he was signed by Bayern Munich in 2019). We lost 1-2, but it was expected because we were playing five or six players without any first-team experience. Diego Rubio scored our goal – it was a very beautiful one – which made me proud. I had spoken with Diego for a bit after a training session, and he didn't have a clue that it was me who had recommended him, but Marc dos Santos was around and he told him. So Diego thanked me because he was very happy there, despite the lack of time on the field. I came back to Portugal happy with my trip, and I felt a great sense of belonging in the SKC world. I felt I was getting the support that I never got at Estoril. It made me feel very motivated.

We managed to qualify for the play-offs but, as had happened the year before, only in the last match of the season, and I wasn't overly confident in the team at the time. Shortly before, we received another huge blow – Diego Rubio had injured his knee, which needed surgery and would take some time to recover. I started to think I was cursed because the two players I had recommended both suffered long-term injuries in their first year, which was surely unusual; luck definitely wasn't on my side.

Our play-off, knock-out round was against Seattle away. We played most of our best 11, and had a good chance of winning the game. Nuno was benched and Kevin Ellis was partnering Besler in the centre. I decided to watch the game even though it was in the middle of the night for me and I had to work the next day – at least it was a Friday so not too bad. Benny Feilhaber was great on the day, and he led the team to a good performance. We were the best team on the night, but in the end Seattle scored, with their super-sub Valdez knocking us out. Some refereeing decisions had been poor, and it was frustrating to lose like that. It was the third year in a row that we were out after the first play-off match. Seattle, just like Portland the previous year, ended up being crowned MLS champions. The preparation for this match must have been brilliant and the pre-match talk from the coaching staff must have been highly motivating. Even our left-back, Seth Sinovic, who didn't always perform well, played the best I have ever seen.

It was time to start again and prepare a strong 2017 squad. It could be an important time for me, and I had to be ready and provide some good suggestions. Apart from the usual leagues I was covering, I added Norway and Sweden, so I delivered a huge file with shadow teams from seven leagues, and I also did extra work on some Italian Serie B teams. I remember November and December 2016 being crazy months for me as I was trying to find more options.

I thought we definitely needed to sign some wingers, as Brad Davis and Justin Mapp were out. Despite a good goalscoring record, Jacob Petersen was also out, and I fully backed this decision because I didn't think he was good enough. A young player called Connor Hallisey wasn't showing any progress, so he was rightly released too. And our best winger, Graham Zusi, was no longer good enough to play in that position, so he would move to right-back. For me this was brilliant news: we would probably solve our right-back issue and sign two or three wingers, which was a position I was more than ready to suggest some good options for.

One of the players we were trying to sign was in my Portuguese shadow team – Gerso Fernandes, a very quick winger with powerful dribbling skills. Kerry had seen him play twice when he came to Portugal back in 2015. I'd been tracking him closely since I started at SKC and I already knew how good he was from my days scouting for Estoril. On 10 December I went to see him play for Belenenses against Marítimo and he scored the only goal of the game. Later that week I learned the deal had been done and Kerry congratulated me! The Portuguese press highlighted the transfer and it was very good for my and SKC's reputation in Portugal. I was very happy that Gerso had joined the 2017 squad, but there was still a lot of work to do. My focus was now totally on the other big gap: we needed a defensive midfielder.

On my favourite players list there were three names who Brian liked a lot: Lorenzo 'Lolo' Reyes, who was an ex-Bétis Sevilla and Almeria player and had gone back to Chile; Joeri de Kamps, a Dutch player from the Ajax youth ranks who was now playing in Slovakia; and Laurent Abergel, whose contract was coming to an end with AC Ajaccio. Later I added Francesco Della Rocca to the list from my extra work on the Italian Serie B, and Kerry liked him a lot; on the other hand he was not a big fan of Abergel so he was out. However, for financial reasons or because of the players themselves, they all became impossible to sign. In the end we signed Spanish player Ilie Sanchez who was not on my list, but I understood that it was the only possible option and the timing was good because he had been out of contract since the summer. I must admit, I didn't sleep well that night knowing he was the player we'd chosen and we hadn't been able to sign one of my choices.

We also signed Latif Blessing, a young winger from Ghana, and Daniel Salloi, a promising young Hungarian winger/forward who was coming back after a loan period. Erik Palmer-Brown was also returning from his time at FC Porto. Our squad was ready for the next season and I was much more confident.

The start of the season was a slow one! In the first four matches, we drew 0-0 three times. And Gerso was pretty average, so I started to feel under pressure. But on 10 April we won 3-1 against Colorado and Gerso scored his first goal for his new club. He bagged another goal versus Real Salt Lake two weeks later and was instrumental in a 2-2 draw versus Orlando away from home. But the magic night came on 18 May! It was a midweek game and I couldn't watch it live but I woke up at around 5.30 in the morning and went to check the score on my mobile phone. The final result was Sporting KC 3 Seattle Sounders 0 – all three goals were scored by Gerso! And the team were now in a very good place in the table, fighting for the lead! The pressure on me subsided and Gerso was now a star amongst the SKC fans.

In January that year, I achieved a bit of a milestone for myself, too – my 100th scouting mission for SKC – and to make it even more special it was at Benfica's stadium. The match was against Boavista and it ended in a 3-3 draw. At that time, and as agreed with Brian, I used to do a tour of Northern Portugal twice a season. It was great to visit Braga's or Guimarães's stadiums for the first time. I love the way football is followed in the north, the crowds of fans are always bigger and there is so much passion.

I finished my season with 62 scouting missions under my belt, which was fewer than in my first season, but I did more video work to compensate for it. My last game of the season was the Portuguese Cup Final, which Benfica won 2-1 against Guimarães. I delivered my shadow teams, which were much more selective, with only two players per position from each league I was covering. I was now stronger in the Italian second tier and I included a page from this league for the first time. Our team was becoming stronger and I wanted to be sure I was making a contribution to it.

A few weeks before the end of the season, Brian told me that the club had decided to increase my wages. I was so happy, not just because of the extra money but also because it was a sign that they were happy with my work and I was doing things right. When I told Patricia, she thought I was kidding, but after realising it was true, she was very happy too. This was proof that I had the quality and knowledge to do a good job as a scout. I was working many more hours than a normal part-time job demands; I was giving it everything I'd got because I was hungry to succeed. This reward made me feel like my efforts had paid off.

Also that year, on 16 March, ESPN wrote an article about scouting in MLS for their website, and after sending me some questions they published some of my responses, which was another proud moment in my career, although I was wrongly quoted about Ilie Sanchez! The article is below:

> Kansas City has taken the approach of employing two foreign scouts, one each in Europe and South America. SKC's man in Europe, Rui Marques, is based in Portugal and covers five leagues in Europe. It was through his efforts that Kansas City signed winger Gerso Fernandes and Spanish midfielder Ilie Sanchez.

'That piece has lent itself well because when he's looking at players, they're not far off or they're really close to what we would be looking for ourselves,' Vermes said.

By Marques' count, he's seen more than 100 games live since he first started working for the club in summer 2015. He's also watched countless others on video. Marques admits sometimes he has trouble sleeping if he's watched too many games in one day, but that overall he finds the work fulfilling. And throughout the years, he's been able to hone his craft in finding potential signings.

'I think the most difficult task for a scout, it's to evaluate if the player does the best decisions during a match,' Marques said via email. 'It is easy to see if a player has shooting or dribbling skills or if he plays with enough intensity and hardness. I think the best scouts should process in their minds accurate information on a quick way when they are observing a match and within that information must be not only the technical aspects but also the ones that fall into the decision-making category.'

18
SPORTING KANSAS CITY 2017/2018 (third season)

I started the new season trying to be innovative. As in the previous year, I had some spare time in June and July as I didn't have any live matches to go to, so I spoke to Brian and asked him which new leagues he thought I should start to follow more on video. We agreed that Switzerland and Poland should be my new ones, and I should drop Sweden and Norway because I didn't get a good reaction from Kerry about the players I had recommended from those leagues. Brian wasn't enthusiastic either, particularly about Norway where he had seen some live games himself.

I was so busy that for a week or so I felt my eyelid flickering. I was a bit worried, I think I was spending too much time watching football on my laptop. I had to slow down a bit so I decided to play tennis more often that summer. We also went to Sesimbra for a holiday and we had some great days at the beach, where Leonardo had a really good time! I have some nice memories of him mimicking and singing Queen songs and he was only three and a half years old.

And it was during this holiday that I decided to start writing a book about my story!

I was asked to look at a possible new player who the club were interested in signing. His name was Cristian Lobato and he was playing in the leagues I was covering, at Nastic Tarragona from the Spanish second tier. He didn't make my shadow team, but I had in fact included him as one of the best options to sign from the work I had done on players whose contracts were coming to an end the year before. After seeing the success of Ilie Sanchez, I thought that Lobato could also be successful and I gave a positive response about his signing. He was a versatile player who could even adapt to playing at left-back. In the summer transfer window he was our only addition to the squad. I also worked hard to find a young, cheap Portuguese defensive midfielder to learn from Ilie, so they would have a reliable alternative, but no deal went ahead.

Gerso and Ilie were both performing above my expectations. Gerso was showing great progress in his finishing, which he had struggled with in the past. And Ilie had established himself as a lynchpin in our system, connecting the midfield, despite not being aggressive enough to be my kind of defensive midfielder. I wrote an email to Kerry to congratulate the coaching staff on the great job they were doing with Ilie and Gerso. The team were doing well in the league and we were also having a good run in the cup. Our B team, Swope Park Rangers, now had Nikola Popovic as the main coach and Kevin Oliveira had started to play again, and he was heading back to his best after such a tough injury. Marc dos Santos left for a new project with a team from the NASL in San Francisco.

In the transfer market in July there was a bit of a surprise – Dom Dwyer our main striker was sold to Orlando City in a record deal for domestic MLS transfers. It was time to find a substitute for him. Diego Rubio was coming back from injury and he was the only natural striker in our squad, as Cameron Porter was injured. I did a quick refresh and started to reorganise my best striker options. It is important for a scout to be quick and provide good solutions in unexpected situations, and I think I did a good job because I came up with some strong and realistic options, but we didn't sign any players in the end. I consoled myself with the fact that Diego Rubio would have an opportunity to show his value as he would finally be the number-one striker.

After suffering a serious injury the year before, Rubio showed great strength and character and worked hard to come back and play at his best. He scored a magnificent goal against Philadelphia in July, followed by another versus San Jose in the cup semis when we booked our place in the final. He scored again against Dallas, with Gerso also adding one for a 2-0 win. Even the Portuguese press noticed it and published a headline saying something like 'two well-known names from Portugal are shining in MLS'. I was proud of 'my boys'. By this time, in August, I was already planning my next annual visit to KC.

For the first time, I had decided to travel with Leonardo and Patricia. I wanted them to experience some of the good things I had done in my previous visits to Kansas City. Patricia was a bit afraid of flying so far with Leonardo, but in the end she decided we should all go together. Since she had become a mother, she hadn't left Portugal but now our son was old enough to behave and enjoy it. My plan was to watch a league game and also the cup final, which would be played at home after being decided by a draw. This was a big risk for me in case we lost such a big game, but it could also be a great moment. When we were onboard the plane,

I took a phone call from Kevin Oliveira's agent who told me that SKC wanted to promote him to the first team! It would be the cherry on top to see Kevin playing for the first team!

As I arrived, the team were preparing for the game against New England Revolution and I watched the last training session before the match. I exchanged a few words with Gerso (and Jimmy Medranda who was with him) and I asked him if he remembered me. He told me, yes, he remembered me 'perfectly'. It was the first time we'd spoken since he'd signed for SKC and I was chuffed that he knew who I was. I told him I was very happy with his performances and I wished them both luck in the next match. I remember reading an interview with a fellow scout once who said it was strange that some players he'd spotted and had been signed by the club he was working for didn't have a clue who he was, and they could cross him in a corridor and wouldn't even look at him. I try to keep a low profile, but I don't see any problems in having a friendly relationship with a player in these circumstances.

17 September 2017 – MLS Match – Sporting Kansas City vs New England Revolution

I asked for tickets so that Patricia and Leonardo could watch the match with me, and we went to the stadium very early. It was their first time so I wanted to show them everything. Despite it being my third time in Kansas City, it was the first time I'd used a hire car, which had been rented for me by the club, so I could plan my schedule without being dependent on anyone else. Patricia was impressed with the stadium's magnificence and beauty. Leonardo was happy playing with some stickers that had our logo and pictures of the players on them, but he was a bit scared of the fireworks before the match! Gerso and Rubio were in the starting 11 and Kevin was on the bench. It had the potential to be a remarkable night.

New England scored very early in the game, just after four minutes, after a lucky deflection. I didn't have time to get nervous because they were down to ten men a few minutes later; Nemeth, our ex-player, being sent off for elbowing Zusi. Then, in the 16th minute Gerso equalised! It was amazing to see how much the supporters loved Gerso. Before going in for half-time, we put ourselves in the lead with an easy goal from Diego Rubio – 2-1! Leonardo was already sleeping by then, but my wife was still enjoying the match and holding him at the same time. I hope she was proud of her husband. We kept control of the game in the second half, adding another goal, again scored by Diego Rubio! And then the cherry on top that I'd been hoping for, Kevin Oliveira came on with 15 minutes to go and played very well. It was a night that was near perfection for me! After the game I complimented Diego Rubio and exchanged a few words with him! He was very happy, and I told him that every time I am in Kansas City he scores!

After the game there was a huge thunderstorm, and I was driving to the hotel on a very dangerous road! I will never forget the fear I had as the rain was so heavy that visibility was terrible. Anyway, we survived and after arriving safe and sound at the hotel I could breathe easy and sleep in peace after a glorious night!

One of the items on my agenda for my trip to KC was the meeting to discuss the 2018 squad. This time it was not as exciting as the previous year and I was much more careful about what I said. Brian showed us some videos he'd edited of some players we were following, including

Yohan Croizet, a French player I had recommended in my shadow teams since November 2015, who was playing for the Belgian team Mechelen, so I was pleased about that.

The day after the meeting, I watched Swope win against San Antonio 5-2 in a match that Nikola told me was probably the best of the season. Was I giving positive energy to everybody? Maybe I was! While I was there, in my spare time I had a memorable day visiting the zoo and I also had time to see 'The Scout' monument. It's a funny coincidence that one of the most well-known monuments in the city is called 'The Scout'.

20 September 2017 – US Open Cup Final – Sporting Kansas City vs New York Red Bulls

The week had been like a fairytale so far, but the big moment was yet to come – the cup final and a trophy were within reach! After watching the team training, I was confident that anything could happen. This time I went to watch the match by myself so that I could be completely focussed, so my family stayed at the hotel. Before the match, I bought some scarves and shirts to give to my friends, I was so excited. I was so proud to get an access-all-areas ticket too, and I was treated with such great respect by the security staff in the stadium. I went to my seat, where I was sitting with Brian, Nikola and Mike. To my left a bit further away were Ashley and Kerry, ready to work and provide information to Peter and Zoran about the players' positions and other details.

This was an all-or-nothing game, and it was a bit of a gamble for me to be there on such a big occasion, in case we lost. But you need to take risks in life. A win would mean a perfect week for me. A defeat would mean disappointment, and my presence would be associated with a sad moment for the club. I know the feeling of being one match away from glory, and I know sometimes we have to suffer before having a moment of glory. I was already working for SKC when we won the MLS Open Cup back in 2015, but this time I was there, watching the game live in the stadium; now it was for real!

As usual, the fans sang the American national anthem before the game. The atmosphere was great. We started a bit better than the opposition, but the match was pretty even. Gerso and Diego Rubio were in the starting 11 – how would they deal with such a big moment for them? They were in good shape and had certainly had a morale boost after their excellent performance four days before.

The game started! The first chance came for Gerso, but he was tackled at the last moment. In the 25th minute, we scored! It was little Latif Blessing who headed in a cross from our great right-back Zusi! Big celebrations followed and we were one step closer to our goal. But a few minutes later we saw the opposition react well with their young midfielder Tyler Adams leading them. They had a few chances to level the score. Minutes before half-time, we made a counter-attack and Gerso was completely free to run and score ... but he missed! I felt some frustration after this wasted opportunity. I thought Gerso looked a bit tense and lost his cool. But we moved into half-time with a 1-0 lead.

We started the second half in control of the game, and as the minutes ticked by I was starting to think it could be our night. Then on the 66th minute a long ball from Benny Feilhaber found our young Hungarian forward, Daniel Salloi, who was smart enough to produce the slightest touch to slide the ball away from the goalkeeper and make it 2-0 for us. I remember an overwhelming feeling of relief. Now it was just a countdown to the party. However, the last minutes were tough, with NYRB's efficient striker Bradley Wright-Phillips scoring, and in the dying seconds a dangerous free kick could have resulted in a draw. But moments later the referee blew the final whistle and we had won 2-1! I complimented my director, Brian Bliss, and I stayed in my seat to enjoy the feeling. They started to play 'We Are The Champions' by Queen in the stadium! It was very emotional to hear Freddie Mercury's voice and it made this moment even more unforgettable and brilliant.

I tried to enjoy the celebrations as much as I could. I went over to the side of the pitch and felt so privileged to see our captain and staff holding up the cup. I recorded these moments with my mobile phone camera. The cup was then put in our locker room and I went there to see if I could hold it and take a photo. There was a big celebration going on in there, with the players leading it, of course. I spoke to Kevin Oliveira, who had played in the last 15 minutes of the game, and he was incredibly happy. I will never forget what he said to me when he was holding the cup: 'Rui, there are things that money can't buy, right?' I agree. Gerso was also enjoying the moment. Brian took a photograph of the celebrations and one of me with the cup. It was the end of a very memorable week.

I started saying my goodbyes as I was going back to Portugal the next morning. Coach Peter Vermes was incredible and gave me a big hug and thanked me for my work – it felt like mission accomplished. Patricia and Leonardo were waiting for me at the hotel. She was still awake and already knew we had won. We both knew it was mission accomplished, and our visit to KC was perfect. It was a magical week and one that we will remember forever. I had some trouble sleeping that night, maybe because my adrenaline levels were so high. Now it was time to travel back to Lisbon and continue my work with even more motivation – our eyes were now on the MLS Cup!

Unfortunately, we didn't finish the season well. Our team fell out of shape after the Open Cup win. I thought we needed a new striker as I didn't think we'd be strong enough to fight for the MLS championship. I think squad depth is very important if a team is going to win something like MLS, and losing such an influential player and not replacing him immediately was always going to put us at a disadvantage. In the end, we qualified for the play-offs but we'd have to play one win-or-bust match away from home – another knock-out round. The match was against Houston Dynamo, and I got up in the middle of the night to watch it. Just like the year before against Seattle, it ended with terrible frustration. It was a very close game, but this time we couldn't complain about the referee; Houston were the better team on that night. Gerso was our best player in the first half but picked up an injury at the start of the second half and was taken off.

I don't always deal well with defeat, and I was in a terrible mood at work the next day. My manager didn't mention it but I remember having no patience with my colleagues. I decided to work on a report about what our priorities should be for 2018 and suggest what had gone wrong at the end of the previous season. I think I took a bit of a risk writing such an honest and critical report, but it was well received and my colleagues agreed with 90 per cent of what I had written. To be honest, I was feeling angry because some TV commentators had said that SKC hadn't found any talent in Europe and that was the reason for their failure. I was the European scout and I didn't think I'd failed. I had always presented good options for every position, and Gerso's first season for SKC had been a great start. Then Diego Rubio had be come the number-one striker after Dwyer left, and his average number of goals per game was higher than his predecessor's. Plus, Kevin Oliveira had made his first-team debut – it seemed a bit unfair to me.

By the end of October we had already done lots of work in preparation for the next MLS season. Brian had been in Europe to watch games in Belgium and Spain. His aim was to see some of the players I had mentioned in my shadow teams and other reports play live. He was happy with most of the players he watched, and in particular Yohan Croizet – a player I had been suggesting since my first season working for SKC, and Brian had been tracking since then too. There had been some conversations with the player's agent and a possible transfer was under discussion.

We needed more options in the attacking midfield position as Benny Feilhaber was nearly 33 years old and had had a poor 2017 season. I was also working hard to come up with options for a defensive or central midfielder and, of course, trying to find a high-profile striker to fill the gap that opened when Dwyer left, despite Diego Rubio performing well.

As the days passed, some decisions were being made. Yohan Croizet was the first to sign, so it was a great start for me. Personally, when I achieve something, I don't lose my focus, I concentrate even more. So, I was even more determined to get another player from my list signed. I was working very hard and I even started to work on videos in the German second tier, as I knew a Portuguese agent who was very strong in that market.

To maximise my chances of getting deals done and to relieve Brian of some work, I started to develop more relationships with agents so I could ask them for information on players who would move to MLS, and the financial aspects, among other things. I could have five or six open discussions at a time with agents from different countries, like Spain, Italy, Germany, Scotland and, of course, Portugal. It was good experience and I learned a lot about how to deal with agents and how they could help me, but I also learned that they could lie to me too. I remember an agent telling me the transfer amount a player would be happy to move for, but when I put the agent in contact with Peter and Brian that amount was much higher! It was disappointing that my efforts had resulted in wasted time and energy for two people who were already working hard to get the best possible players for our team.

I was working so hard and felt very tired by the time Christmas and New Year came – my lowest moment was the night of my work Christmas dinner when I was so tired and had such a heavy head that I couldn't enjoy it and I was probably close to total burnout.

A number of opportunities were opening up at the club and we signed two great players: Johnny Russell, a Scottish winger who left Derby County – a team that were fighting for promotion to the Premier League – and Felipe Gutierrez – a Chilean international who was having a hard time in Brazil but who had great versatility as he could play in all the midfield positions. A central defender from my list was also nearly signed, but in the end Emiliano Amor, a young

Argentinian defender already on loan from Velez Sarsfield, was signed instead.

So, we were ready for MLS 2018, even though signing a new striker had again been put on hold – a decision that was starting to upset me because I just couldn't understand why. However, for the third year in a row, a new player had joined the squad after being recommended by me. I didn't have a player in the Swope Park Rangers team this time though, and Kevin Oliveira had left the club and signed for a USL team in Canada. It hadn't been possible to reach an agreement with the player's agent, Paulo Teixeira. It was a bit of a blow for me. I tried to help both parties as much as I could, but in the end I couldn't do anything about it.

I followed our pre-season matches with great anticipation, and Brian kept me updated about how well Croizet was adapting to his new club. He did well and earned a place in the first 11 against New York City at home – the first official match of the 2018 MLS season, which started in March as usual. A big surprise in that game was that Gerso was on the bench after he'd done so well in 2017. I watched the match live on Eurosport, and it was a terrible 2-0 defeat, with NY City clearly the better team. Croizet made an impressive move to escape the defenders and managed to appear in front of goal and shoot first time, but it went wide. Apart from that, it was a disappointing performance for him. Diego Rubio didn't play well either and was taken off after 60 minutes. We had to come out fighting in the next game, which was away vs Chicago Fire. The coach, who is usually patient and resistant to changes for the sake of it, decided to bench Croizet, Gerso and Rubio. I saw the team sheet on television and thought that was probably my lowest moment since working for SKC, having all my players on the bench. The game was epic though, with the team starting well and taking a 2-0 lead, but Chicago responded by scoring three goals in the second half. When everything seemed lost, we found the strength to react and scored two late goals to get a 3-4 win! Felipe Gutierrez and Johnny Russell were our best players and that was the start of a long run without defeats, with those two players leading the team.

A month later, Gutierrez picked up an injury and Croizet had a second chance to return to the starting line-up. But again, he didn't perform as well as I knew he could. Week after week, it was painful to watch his performances. He didn't keep possession of the ball or work well with his team-mates, his passes were poor, and he was a shadow of the player he'd been in his last three seasons in Belgium. More disappointment for me.

March 2018

In March I went to Spain on a scouting mission for the first time. I spoke to Brian and presented him with a plan that would see me go to Galicia, a region in the northwest, so I could watch four good matches in just two days, including two from Spain's La Liga. We still needed strikers and I would be able to check out some potentially excellent options for us.

On Saturday, 17 March I went to watch Deportivo La Coruña against Las Palmas. I took some photos before the match – I was so happy to be there watching one of the best leagues in the world live for the first time. I had a bit of a walk to get there as I parked my car a bit far from Riazor, but I did it on purpose so I could see the fantastic Riazor beach, a beautiful bay near the stadium. I focussed my attention on Florian Andone and Lucas Perez from Depor and Jonathan Calleri from Las Palmas. The final score was 1-1 so the strikers were not the stars of the game, but I still left with a positive impression of my targets. Both teams remained in a dangerous position in the table on the verge of relegation. Because of this, it was worth tracking these players as the odds of us being able to sign them in May before our first transfer window closed were much higher.

I then went to watch Lugo vs Alcorcon in the afternoon – a second-division match, but still very exciting and intense after a late comeback from the home team. On Sunday I had two Celta Vigo matches to watch, first the B team, which was, as usual, made up of younger players, then later the main squad who were hosting a struggling team close to being relegated – Malaga. I was not blessed with lots of goals in this Galicia trip, but even the scoreless draw between Celta and Malaga was certainly very exciting. Watching these four matches made me realise that the Portuguese leagues were far below the level of the Spanish competition in all the tiers that I watched. I travelled back to Portugal feeling positive.

When May arrived again no strikers were signed and the search was still on ready for the next transfer window, which would open around 10 July. But the team were still on a high, chasing the top spots and grabbing important away wins – including one against Ibrahimovic's LA Galaxy and another against Atlanta United, one of the rare matches in which Croizet was influential after a good breaking pass that ended in a red card for the Atlanta goalkeeper. I delivered my final shadow teams for my third season at SKC in April/May – I was now covering eight leagues, which I think was my limit considering I had another full-time office job on top of this. One of my last matches of the season was the Portuguese Cup Final between Sporting and Aves. It was my 200th live match as a scout for SKC – an amazing achievement for me in one of the most emblematic stadiums in Portugal – the National Stadium – which I have captured in a photograph which means a lot to me. This match ended with a surprise win for Aves, with a great performance from Carlos Ponck, a player I have mentioned before as I spotted him in a third-tier team when he was a completely unknown player. It was a pleasure to see Quim, the Aves goalkeeper and Portuguese international player, at his peak and ending his career with a cup in his hands. It was one of the great and well-deserved success stories in football, and at 41 years old, after so many highs and lows, he was rewarded with a happy ending!

The 2018 World Cup in Russia was just around the corner. For the first time in my life I'd be following this major competition not only as a fan but also as a professional scout, so I was working and having fun at the same time – a great combination. Four years before, I had been a scout for Estoril, but I didn't think they would be able to sign a player who was part of the World Cup. This time I was watching the games while keeping possible future players for SKC in mind. Sadly, the USA team were not there so there weren't any current SKC players, like Besler or Zusi, representing our club as they had at the 2014 World Cup in Brazil. I thought that maybe Messi would lead Argentina to glory, but after seeing France's performance in their second match of the tournament against Peru, I thought they were the team to beat. When the teams faced each other and France won 4-3, I told my friends that France would win it for sure.

19

SPORTING KANSAS CITY – 2018/2019 (fourth season)

In the same week the World Cup finished, the MLS transfer window opened and I had a good chat with Brian about what we'd need to strengthen the squad. The team was having a bit of a downhill struggle after some heavy defeats, conceding a high number of goals. Strikers were not our only focus now, we also had to consider possibilities for a new central defender and a left-back – we had a lot of injuries as well, our most significant one being Jimmy Medranda, our best option at left-back, even though he was more powerful attacking than defending.

By the middle of July, the European transfer market had already been open for almost two months, so some of the players I thought were good options were already gone, as they had already changed teams or renewed their contracts. But it was my job to find solutions and I couldn't afford to lose any time complaining, so I did some quick research and prepared a shortlist of left-backs who could be immediate options. I wasn't as worried about a central 4defender as Brian told me we had a very good chance of signing a high-profile player from Spain's La Liga to play in that position.

I was able to get some immediate responses about possible targets from the agents I had built relationships with as my career had progressed. I made some enquiries and got a few names who were available at a reasonable price. I was also trying to come up with some new striker options. Less than two days before the deadline I was told Krisztian Nemeth was returning to the club from New England Revolution. After departing SKC for Qatar at the end of 2015, he was struggling to get back to his best. But if our coaching staff could restore his confidence, he would be a massive signing and our attacking line would be strengthened. It was also confirmed that Andreu Fontás, a central defender from Celta Vigo, would replace Emiliano Amor, who hadn't performed well in a number of games and was returning to Argentina. I hadn't had any influence on these two signings and I felt that my recommendations had basically been ignored. I could write an entire chapter about strikers and central defenders I have recommended that I thought were very smart deals, but in the end my vision wasn't shared. It was another huge blow for my work, but I was getting more used to it.

After a terrible run of six games with five defeats and a home draw, the team were eliminated from the Open Cup after a terrible 2-4 defeat at Houston. I was starting to lose hope. After that, we had two away games, first against Houston Dynamo, but this time in the league, and then at Los Angeles FC – a new team where my friend Marc dos Santos was now an assistant coach. Finally, fortune was on our side and we were able to turn things around with two great away wins. At Houston, Gianluca Busio was in the starting 11 for the first time, at only 17 years old, and with 15 minutes remaining, Diego Rubio was played through by Busio and finished with class – just five minutes after coming on from the bench – to give us a 1-0 win. Then against LA FC, Rubio, who played from the start, assisted Gerso and we took an early lead. They gave each other a big celebratory hug, which made me feel proud from the other side of the ocean. The win was the most important thing, but seeing such an important goal being created by my two first signings for SKC was a really great moment for me. They had faced some difficulties earlier in the season, being benched for a number of games, but they showed great character and continued their work to find a place back in the team. I was proud of my boys! We won 2-0 and we were back in the top two in the Western Conference!

For Croizet, the season was still disappointing. He scored what was probably our goal of the season in the 89th minute against Dallas in a memorable 3-2 win in the Open Cup with a fantastic shot outside the area. But it was not a turning point for him, and he didn't find the confidence to play at his best, with the season already entering the final third. There were a lot of comments online from SKC supporters saying his signing had been a poor decision, and I had to agree with them; the way he was playing was not good enough for MLS.

I took two weeks' leave from my full-time job in the second half of August and on some of those days I had planned to spend my time working in Spain, attending two matches in the second division. My schedule would allow me to visit Almendralejo – a western town, where a newly promoted team called Extremadura was hosting Deportivo La Coruña – plus Cordoba and Granada, cities more to the south. The days were very hot over there, with temperatures above 40 degrees. I took a taxi to one of the games, and when I explained my job to the driver he said that I had a fascinating career, which made me realise how lucky I was to be doing this.

I woke up the next day after my trip to Spain to find that SKC had won 2-0 against Minnesota, but more importantly for me Yohan Croizet had been a key player in the win! He came on at the beginning of the second half and scored the first goal after a classy move and finish! Finally, he had shown something I knew he had in his game, and he helped the team get a very important result. Diego Rubio scored the other goal, adding it to the two goals he scored in the previous match against Portland Timbers. What a month he'd had – four goals in four matches, plus one assist! And at the beginning of September he scored again in our defeat at Seattle, which sadly broke our run of four wins. After so much time and energy had been spent trying to find a new striker, it was Diego Rubio who was emerging as the best when we really needed it. My painstaking research for more than a year to find a striker to substitute Dwyer had been wasted, but ironically my boy Diego Rubio offered me a sweet taste of reward! I felt even more proud and happy for Diego when he received a call up for the Chilean national team in September! He deserved it, after seven years without a call up he was there again, playing amongst the best players in his country.

More importantly, though, the team found their winning ways again and we were chasing the top spot in the Western Conference. The last months of the regular season went very well and we made it to the last match of the season, which was at home against LA FC, just needing a draw to win the Western Conference. We did our job and won 2-1, and we ended that match with just ten players after our left-back Sinovic was sent off for a questionable handball. For the first time since I started working for the club, we went directly into the play-off quarter-finals! Exciting days were ahead, for sure!

Our first play-off opponents were Real Salt Lake away from home. To my surprise, our coaching staff decided to play Yohan Croizet as left-back! I knew he was a versatile player, but I had never seen him play in that position. I felt under pressure because it was a big risk and if Croizet failed to perform it could mean our early exit from the competition. I wasn't able to watch the match live, but I woke up in the middle of the night and went to check the final result: 1-1 – not bad! From reading the summary of the match, I knew that Diego Rubio had come on from the bench and scored after only 40 seconds on the field, and supporters and journalists were reporting that Croizet had had a good match. So, I was happy with our start and hopeful that we could do the business in the second leg at home.

I was nervous in anticipation of the match to come. It was broadcast live in Europe at a reasonable time, so all my friends were able to watch it. Even my son was excited about the game and dressed in the club's shirt to show his support. Diego Rubio was in our starting 11, and he helped the team get off to a great start as we were 2-0 up before the 20-minute mark. Rubio scored one and Felipe Gutierrez got the other. We were dominating and it looked like the win would be easy. However, the second half was much more balanced and the opposition got a goal back. But we answered it with another goal and restored our two-goal cushion after a penalty earned by Rubio and scored by Ilie. They fought back again and scored another to make it 3-2 in the last 15 minutes. I was anxious because if they scored another goal it would mean we were out, and they were so close at least three times. But then in the last minute of stoppage time we scored in a counter-attack and finished it. I felt a great sense of relief, but I thought we'd had luck on our side. We had everything we needed to put in a solid performance but we weren't able to do it. We had to improve in the game against Portland Timbers, our semi-final opponents. But we were still in the final four to chase the championship.

We had a two-week break before our first match at Portland, and I was already working with Brian on our team for next season. Our main target was a left-back, and one of my suggestions from Portugal was getting a unanimous 'yes' from all the coaching staff. I had spent a great deal of time using my contacts to get the deal done, so I was doing more than the role of scout. In the end, the player didn't accept our offer for personal reasons. We tried to reach an agreement, and we waited for around three weeks for a final decision, but it was still a 'no'. It was frustrating but we had to live with it, and even before getting the final answer I was already working on more possible options, shifting my focus to the French Ligue 2, where I thought there would be a good option.

The day of the first leg of our semi-final against Portland arrived. It wasn't an exciting match and they were the better team on the day. In the end it was a 0-0 draw away from home and we were favourites going into the second leg. I had already been invited to travel to the USA by the club to watch the final if we reached it. I started to imagine the trip to Atlanta, who were expected to be our opponents in the big final if things went as expected. The final would be played on 8 December, and it would work perfectly as I could travel on the 7th and wouldn't miss my son's birthday the day before. I was so confident that I started looking at things to do in Atlanta to make the most of my short stay there. I thought that maybe I could attend an NBA match there as it is something I'd always wanted to do.

30 November 2018 – Sporting Kansas City vs Portland Timbers, semi-final, second leg

The match was due to start at 2.30am local time for me. It is very hard to stay awake all night, so I decided to go to bed as normal at around 11pm, and if I woke up in the middle of the night I could always restart the match from the beginning without having found out the score. That was my plan, but in the end I woke up naturally exactly 15 minutes before the game started! So, I was ready to go, and I was so excited. I remember telling a friend that this would be the match of my life. It would be amazing to reach the MLS Cup Final. You can love and support a football team, but because I worked for them it was a stronger feeling than I had ever experienced before.

The game started and we took control of the match, and at around 20 minutes we took the lead, Diego Rubio assisting Salloi for an easy tap-in goal. We continued to play well and create chances but couldn't add another. At half-time I was tense, but held on to the fact that we were just 45 minutes away from reaching the final. But, in the first 15 minutes of the second half, Portland scored twice. Their best players, Blanco and Valeri, put their names on the scoreboard. Our coach brought Gerso on and we started to fight back. With ten minutes to go, Gerso levelled the score after a cool finish inside the area. It was anybody's game. At this stage I was already starting to doubt we could win it, but I had to keep the faith until the last minute. But as we were risking everything in the attack, it was Portland that got the final goal of the game in the last minute of stoppage time after a counter-attack, and they booked their place in the final. The dream had turned into a nightmare. I managed to sleep for a couple of hours after but couldn't get over it the next day, I felt a sense of loss and emptiness. It was the worst state I'd been in emotionally because of a football match – ever. I was mentally down when Benfica lost a European final or experienced a heavy defeat, but that was nothing compared to this. I was not prepared to lose, and I knew this had been a key moment for me and my scouting career. In the end, Atlanta United won the trophy, beating Portland Timbers 2-0 in the final.

After some tough days, I managed to overcome these negative feelings and I did some deep analysis of the season. What went wrong? What did we do well? The three players I had recommended who'd been signed ended the season on a high: Diego Rubio scored twice with one assist in the three play-off games he played in, and he also had an impressive scoring ratio, with ten goals from 11 starts, a ratio only beaten by Josef Martinez from Atlanta United and equal to Zlatan Ibrahimovic from LA Galaxy; Gerso Fernandes was our best player in our last match, and his impact in that game was terrific – overall he scored six goals with five assists; and Yohan Croizet was disappointing in the first half of the season but played a key part in our success from August – he started to perform well and scored crucial goals in two important wins, and he showed versatility by performing well at left-back in our first play-off match.

As always, I was now ready to start research in the close season so I could offer some options to the club. My priority was again the left-back position. I suggested lots of quality players but in the end the coaching staff decided to sign a free agent from Costa Rica called Rodney Wallace, who wasn't a left-back but the plan was to adapt him. I was a bit upset by this decision, as I'd been told to focus my scouting work on players who were less than 1.8m tall and no more than 26 years old and he was neither, but I couldn't let it get me down.

Some days later, I received some more surprising and quite painful news – my boy Diego Rubio was sold to Colorado Rapids for $300,000 plus another player. I was so disappointed by this and found it hard to understand the reasons for this decision, it was a bitter pill to swallow.

January 2019

I tried to find some motivation to continue working for SKC. I told Brian at the beginning of the month that for the first time in more than three and a half years I'd lost my enthusiasm. I didn't have the courage to say I wanted to leave but in the end my relationship with the club ended anyway, and I think it was for the best. They offered me a contract in 2019 that had some clauses in it that didn't make sense to me, so I refused to sign. I didn't want to be part of SKC anymore and the Diego Rubio scenario on top of that meant there was only one solution – we had to part ways and I needed to start a new chapter in my life.

I left the club knowing that I'd done a great job and had made a contribution improving the team. In the last five years the team only won one MLS play-off round, against Real Salt Lake in 2018, and the only player to score in both home and away matches was Diego Rubio. So, if there was no place for him in the club in 2019, there was also no place for me either. But, despite this bitter end, I will always be grateful to Peter and Kerry for giving me the opportunity to work with SKC.

SKC's first official match of the 2019 season was also the first one after my departure and it showed that my work for the club had been fruitful: Sporting Kansas City won 3-0 against Deportivo Toluca (Mexico) in the first leg of the CONCACAF Champions League and guess who was man of the match? Gerso Fernandes! He scored a goal, assisted in another and was also key in the third goal! He was also key in the second leg, scoring another goal to help SKC to advance to the quarters. Now, finally being played from the start in almost all the matches, he was the 'maestro' of a 7-1 MLS match win against Montreal Impact, providing two assists in the first half. It is good to leave some kind of legacy behind. About Diego Rubio, it was a remarkable fact that he scored his first MLS goal with his new team Colorado Rapids against Sporting Kansas City to help them to get a point for a 1-1 draw. I have left my mark at MLS. It's good to leave some kind of legacy behind!

20

IMMEDIATELY – A NEW CHALLENGE IS BORN: LEGIA WARSAW!

From the day Diego Rubio was traded I decided that I needed to start looking for a new club. When my inevitable move from SKC became official, I already had some alternative options in the pipeline. I felt unemployed for less than 24 hours, while I was waiting for what turned out to be a very promising phone call.

The story started back in the spring of 2015 when I sent my CV to some Polish clubs, as I wanted to leave Estoril and I had planned to spend a week in Poland. A scout from Legia Warsaw called Radoslaw Kucharski (Radek) replied and we started to develop a friendship. He worked for Manchester United in 2016, but he came back to Legia, where he is now the technical director. We met in October when he came to Portugal on a scouting mission. As Legia were in Portugal for a training camp because the league was on a winter break, Radek called me to invite me to visit them at Troia, in January 2019, a beautiful place an hour away from my home. I told him that I had recently left SKC and I was now looking for a new club. The timing was perfect, and we scheduled a meeting for the next day.

I took a day off from my full-time job and travelled first by car to Setubal (less than an hour from my town) and then I went by ferry to Troia. When I was on the boat I remembered that last time I had been interviewed, which was for SKC, I'd had to go to Madrid so this would be an improvement as it is much closer to my home town. The meeting lasted for a couple of hours and I thought it went OK. After the meeting, me and Radek went to the Legia training session, which I really enjoyed.

Two weeks later, Radek called me and told me that they wanted to hire me, and an agreement would be sent to me soon! After a few more days of waiting for a couple of details to be ironed out, Radek told me I had access to Wyscout and could officially start work for Legia! From the day that SKC cancelled my Wyscout login until I got a new account with Legia, I have to say I felt some sense of emptiness and that something was missing in my daily life. When the 25-day wait was over it was like breathing again!

My new club are the current Polish champions and the immediate goal is to win the title again. Currently we are in second place, with Lechia Gdansk leading the table. The history of the club is very rich and my first memory of them is when, back in the 1990/91 season, they reached the Cup Winners' Cup semi-final, losing only to Manchester United, who went on to win the competition that season. The stadium has a capacity of around 30,000 and the supporters are amazing. The most famous player in the club's history is Kazimierz Deyna, a great attacking midfielder who also helped the Polish national team reach third place in the 1974 World Cup. He played more than 300 matches for Legia over 12 years before moving to Manchester City.

Ironically, my first scouting match in the Champions League in 2016 was Sporting CP hosting versus Legia Warsaw! Also, in the current Legia squad there are three players who I recommended to SKC in the past: a young defender called Mateusz Wieteska, a Portuguese winger called Iuri Medeiros and the Spanish striker Carlitos Lopez.

My first complete month – March 2019 – with Legia was frenetic! I have watched 14 live matches in three different countries! From Le Havre (France) to Almeria (Spain), I had been in lots of places doing scouting missions! A great start with my scouting career moving to another dimension!

I believe in myself and in my talent and I will keep on trying and fighting to achieve my own goals within the football world. I am more than a fantasy football winner, I am a scout who is building a successful career – that might sound arrogant but, yes, I think I am!

21

THE ART OF SCOUTING

Sometimes I think to myself, how would I describe the perfect scout? Like the perfect football player (or coach), you need to analyse it from both qualitative and quantitative points of view.

When I am asked to suggest players for a certain position with a given profile, if I am able to present a number of players rather than one or two that means I have done a better job. So, from a quantitative point of view, it is important for a scout to retain as much information as possible and cover the largest range of players that he can. In my career so far, I have been able to progressively expand the number of leagues I cover. If I am asked to suggest a player for a certain position, the quicker I can provide good answers and the more solutions I can offer, the better scout I am. Nowadays, I am much more efficient in providing what I am asked for.

However, it is not just about the number of players I suggest. Of course, it's important to remember a good number of players from my recent assessments, but I also need to keep quality standards high by evaluating them thoroughly. I can't produce a complete evaluation of a player after seeing him once and memorising what he did in that game. Although I rely heavily on my instincts to decide a player's value, I must see him enough to give him my 'quality seal'. One thing that all scouts know is that our margin of error is much lower when we are in the stadium rather than using video. However, I believe I can still be completely right about a player even if I've never seen him play live.

A good scout should know how to evaluate a player's basic skills, such as whether he is fast or has good technique, but he must also identify the little details. When I say details, I mean something that the player did which shows he is above average, that he is special, something that is unusual to see at the level he is playing. It is extremely important for a scout to understand if a player chooses wisely when he has a number of options available to him in any given moment during a game. A good example of this is in a counter-attack when a player must decide and execute his move quickly but has enough space to consider several possible options. Quick and correct decision-making is one of the most important skills to assess in a player, and it is perhaps the hardest one to see, as we have to understand the decisions of the player with the ball, but also the decisions of all the others taking part in the play at the time. We only have two eyes so video analysis is an important extra tool to help in making the correct assessment.

Basically, I evaluate a player in four main areas: technical, physical, psychological, tactical. On top of this, I have to assess two more things: consistency of the player and their pace. All these different areas must be assessed together. Let's not forget that a player can have some physical limitations but at the same time be smart enough to disguise it. Two good examples of this are: a light striker who is clever enough to avoid contact with the defenders or a slow defender who is smart enough to position himself so that he doesn't give the opposition a chance to beat him. I will give more importance to each area depending on the player's position; for example, I don't mind if a central defender is less technical but has enough intelligence and thinks fast enough to make sure he is not caught with the ball when under pressure. I also don't care if a winger is not very tall if he has enough pace and dribbling power to shake a defender one on one. It is also possible to overate a player because of the way he looks, for example if he appears elegant or good-looking. I have noticed some colleagues underrate players who are bald or walk differently. What I am certain of is that I only want players who are consistent or can play with the necessary pace for the game.

It is fundamental to know how to rank players. If player A is good and player B is also very similar, I must be able to decide which one is better because in the end the team with the best players will win even if the quality of the players is very close. It's not enough to say that a player is 'good' because it will always depend on your perspective. A player could be good for Team X but not good enough for Team Y. Or player Z is good, but player W is better. If I must decide yes or no to one or the other one, I need to be able to make the decision and be right. I usually deliver my choices in my shadow teams, but I also build a file that I call 'Rankings', where I will put the top-five players for each position within the leagues I cover.

A great scout will find value in a player and know that he is good enough to perform at a higher level than he is currently playing at, at least playing to the same standard. It is also important to know how to rank the leagues against each other, understanding their level in comparison to the league of the club you are working for. And before doing an assessment it's important to be clear if the player was really tested or not. Were the opponents too easy for him? Did the game have enough difficult moments to see if the player is really any good?

There are other questions that I ask myself before recommending a player: What phase of his career is he in? Is he already declining? Is it the right time for them to play abroad? Is he an injury-prone player? Does he have a good mentality on and off the field? Is he hungry for a new project? Sometimes we can't find the answers so we have to take risks.

I also have to keep in mind what my team coaches like and what type of play they usually apply. A coach can prefer a defensive midfielder who is more constructive than a destroyer. Or they may prefer full-backs who can be very powerful attacking rather than stronger defending. Sometimes we have to go against our own opinions and ideas because in the end the most important thing is that the team wins.

When I am on a scouting mission and not focussed on a specific player, I usually try to look out for players who show strength or are an asset to their team. I also have to be aware that a player might not be having a good game because he is missing something but is still close to delivering. If I think he is close, I'll track him because he may deliver soon, or he might deliver for another team in a different competitive context. It is quite common to see a player play well even though their team didn't score or conceded too many goals. A team could be last in the table and conceding too many goals, but they could still have an excellent defender. I never exclude the possibility of finding a diamond in a very weak team.

The structure of my reports about players is quite simple, but it has all the essential information. I split it up into strengths and weaknesses, plus analysis and assessment. You can see below an example of a report I wrote in 2017 for a player (Alex Pasche) from the Swiss league who was a good option for SKC at the time, and for a fair price.

In summary, I think a good scout has the ability to suggest a number of players, and the assessments for those players will always be recent and complete. However, this is still completely subjective and only the player's performance in the future will validate the report. And a scout's performance, just like a player or a coach, must be measured by their results.

When I put my 'quality seal' on a certain player and he is not hired, I make a point of pursuing his career to validate my own assessment. If he is hired, it puts me under pressure and the player's performance will determine whether I have performed well or not. I have already recommended successful players, but I've also got it wrong. But, in my opinion, I am as good as the ratio of my successes to failures. Some scouts could always make the excuse that the coaching staff were not good enough to get the best out of the player, but the same coaching staff may be capable of getting the best out of other players recommended, so a scout must always share part of a failure if it doesn't work out.

Another interesting thing to think about is that a scout can be very confident in a certain player's ability, but the asking price is not fair. If this occurs, I like to take the role of asset manager for the club if I can. If I suggest a player

Alex PASCHE

Main Position: Central Midfielder
Born: 31 May 1991
Height: 5 ft 9 in
Foot: Right

Team: Lausanne (Switzerland)
Nationality: Swiss
Scouting Matches Focus: Apr/Jun 17

STRENGTHS

- Ability to RECOVER the ball showing very good TACKLING skills. Wins a good percentage of the LOOSE BALLS duels, playing always with competitive ATTITUDE, DETERMINATION and ENERGY.

- Responsible with BALL POSSESSION, rarely loses it. Plays with efficient SHORT PASSES, based on simple and quick touches, helping to ORGANISE the midfield and to set up team movements. Right footed but his left foot is reasonable.

- OFF THE BALL initiatives are part of his natural game, offering a passing line for his team players frequently, doing diagonal runs.

- Develops his action through an EXTENSIVE AREA, progresses well with the ball and can go to the wings and have 1x1 movements doing CROSSES (he is also a corner kick taker) with reasonable quality for a central midfield player.

WEAKNESSES

- Shows difficulties on AERIAL DUELS, mainly because his height is below average. He also has some troubles when having more physical battles for the ball with much taller players.

- Misses the LAST and KEY PASS very often, maybe lacking CONFIDENCE but also revealing TECHNICAL limitations. He can run fast with the ball and lead a counter-attack but his DECISION-MAKING under pressure is not always the best.

- Even knowing that he is not an attacker he should appear more on FINISHING positions and score more goals.

ANALYSIS

A player aged 26 years that built all his career so far in Switzerland but never played for a top team that could be dominant and impose attacking authority on the game (like SKC does). In my opinion he is an underrated player because his overall package of skills, namely his strong mentality and hard work ratio, would result in developing the potential of his game and improving some weak aspects (gaining some key passing confidence) of his game if he played in a better team. I justify also my opinion because it is interesting to notice that when he plays against better teams (Basel or Young Boys) on a higher tempo, he responds well and is more consistent. Defensively he is competent and offers lots of solutions (apart from aerial duels).

ASSESSMENT

Perspective vs SKC 2017 roster – He can chase a regular starter spot in our team as a central midfielder (position 8). He can also perform well as a defensive midfielder for us, adding more aggression but keeping quality passing/organisation level. With his multitasking profile he is a player that would add depth and make our roster more solid which is in my opinion a key condition to win competitions.

Rating : 6.95 out of 10.

but the cost involved is exaggerated and doesn't make sense, I have no problem in removing him from my list.

It is also important to manage emotions if you are frustrated when a player you are confident will succeed is rejected by the coaching staff. Throughout this book I have mentioned my disappointments. Again, just like a player or a coach has to face frustration during the season, a scout must be able to cope with it and be resilient too. All the experiences we have and all the knowledge we absorb can always be useful in the future. Opportunities will present themselves, and we just need to be ready to grab them.

A scout must try to be perfect, and he must also find the perfect club to work for. The perfect team to work with is one that trusts their scout's assessments and who will move fast to sign the player, knowing they will perform at a higher level than they are currently playing at. If I go back to 2016, there are two players in my shadow team that are perfect examples of this, but they were ignored. Firstly, Ferland Mendy was a 20-year-old left-back, playing for Le Havre (French Ligue 2), who was coming to the end of his contract and was not the team's first option. However, he played a few games when the usual left-back wasn't fit and he performed very well and impressed me, so I took the risk of putting him in my shadow team above many other players who played more matches than him within that league. Today, Mendy is the first-option left-back for Olympique Lyon and was recently called up for the French national team. Secondly, Birger Meling was 22 years old, playing for Stabaek (Norway), also a left-back, who I selected as my first option in my Norwegian shadow team in 2016 – today he is at Rosenborg and was offered to us in November 2018 for a transfer fee of $2.5 million.

Sometimes I feel like I'm seeing things that nobody else sees. I might have an opinion about a player that nobody else agrees with. However, if you double-check whether you are right or not, it's not a problem if you often turn out to be right. I don't like to be stubborn and will change my opinion, but I don't think it's a good sign if you are wrong most of the time and others are right – that probably means you're in the wrong job! It's true that a scout can't always predict the future, but the ones who are better at foreseeing what will happen next are generally the best.

I have challenged myself to build my top-five best scouting assessments. My main criteria was to analyse the competition level of the player when I spotted him and where he is now. That's not easy because I had to exclude a long list of good ones, such as Anderson Esiti, Piatek, Krovinovic, Gabriel Appelt, Dyego Sousa, Andy Delort, Toko Ekambi, Bruno Jordão or Dalbert. But anyway, here goes:

5 – NABY KEITA

I was watching a French Ligue 2 game on my laptop, trying to find good players for Estoril. The streaming was not very high quality, but I spotted a young Guinean player playing for Istres, a struggling team. After that I decided to track him, and he built a successful career. Nowadays, he is a Liverpool player and is worth millions.

4 – SERGIO LEON

I was researching central defenders for SKC on video, watching matches from the previous season in the summer of 2015 in my early scouting days for the club, and I noticed an interesting striker playing for Llagostera. He was later signed by Elche and I included him in my Spanish second-tier shadow team. Now he is a respected striker for Betis Sevilla, valued at around €5 million.

3 – DIEGO RUBIO

As I have mentioned before, I knew him well from Sporting B and I knew that he could be successful in MLS. He was having a hard time on the bench at Valladolid in the second tier in Spain and I decided to suggest him to SKC. He was signed and had a great season in 2018, contributing a lot to the club's success with his goalscoring ability.

2 – CARLOS PONCK

I will never forget my surprise and excitement when, at a Portuguese third-tier match, I noticed a young defensive midfielder who was powerful and knew how to play simply and efficiently. He was always present in my shadow teams. Benfica signed him but loaned him to other teams, but he is now a regular starter at Aves who are in the Portuguese first division, and he is getting better every game.

1 – STEPHEN EUSTÁQUIO

I spotted this player at a Portuguese third-tier match when he was just 19 and I recommended him to SKC when they asked for a young and cheap midfielder as a back-up. Nowadays, at just 21 years old, he is already a starter in the first division with Chaves and is a Portugal under-21 international. He was being followed by high-profile teams in Spain and England but ended up signing for Cruz Azul, a Mexican team, for £3 million for 50 per cent of the future rights. Unfortunately, he picked up an injury in one of his first matches!

PART IV: PERSPECTIVES

22
FOOTBALL TODAY: MY VIEWS

In my opinion, football is the best sport ever and the most entertaining show on the planet. Every four years, when the World Cup is on, I try to rearrange my life so that I can enjoy it to the full. I still think it's a competition that has been able to keep a lot of the magic and the passion that football can bring. Every four years we watch new stories unfold that will stay in our memory for the rest of our lives. It's a competition where Senegal can beat France or South Korea can beat Germany. An unexpected star can be born; it could be a Roger Milla, a Kylian Mbappé or a Toto Schillaci, we never know. And it seems likely that more African and Asian countries will be able to compete in this competition in the near future. FIFA are trying to bring more countries to the party.

But, unfortunately, nowadays there are lots of things within the football industry that I don't agree with. It's sad that every year we already know that the UEFA Champions League Final will be played between teams from the big-four countries: Spain, England, Germany and Italy. Although, eventually PSG from France will get there too with the financial power they have now. I learned to love this sport in the 80s, and the pinnacle of each season was the European Cup Final, which is the equivalent of the Champions League Final today. But at the time, this match could be played by a team from a much wider variety of countries, such as Romania, Serbia, Portugal or the Netherlands. I have watched some teams from these countries win the trophy in brilliant matches. But now UEFA have created a system where the rich countries win everything, and year after year they become richer.

What will football be like in the future, 50 years from now, if nothing changes? Will Real Madrid already have 30 Champions League trophies in their museum? Or will Barcelona have clinched their 20th trophy? Surely Bayern Munich, Juventus or Atletico Madrid will have won some as well. And the top teams in England will grab a few.

But historical European teams like Ajax, PSV Eindhoven, Feyenoord, Celtic Glasgow, SL Benfica, FC Porto, Steaua Bucharest and Red Star Belgrade will only reach a final if there is a miracle. Is this a fair system? Does this make any sense? Since 2004, when FC Porto won against Monaco of Deschamps under Mourinho, only teams from the big-four countries have reached the final.

The political and economic concept of the European Union is based on the increase of equality and cohesion among the member states, but in terms of football it's completely the opposite. The UEFA Champions League model is in need of a change, starting with the allocation of matches in the Group phase. The big-four countries will already have four teams qualified for this phase, while champions of countries like Poland or Serbia must knock out four teams and play eight matches before getting there. Of course, this will cause the gap to increase year after year, because if some countries start with four teams and others struggle to get one team in the group stage, we can't expect anything other than the results we see now.

I think that fans from Madrid who, year after year, see two of their country's teams fighting for the European championship are just as important as are the fans from Malta, Albania or Iceland, who unfortunately don't have a chance of seeing their teams play against teams from the most powerful nations. How can football in these countries evolve if the system doesn't allow them to play a single match against the big teams?

Football can't only be about business! The priority can't only be to generate revenue and limit the chances of victory to teams from just four countries, making the competition quite exclusive.

Even for the Spanish fans, it is becoming ridiculous: there are seasons when Barcelona win the league and the cup, but Real Madrid win the Champions League, so do Barça fans consider the season frustrating? Bayern Munich and Juventus are the only teams in the fight because of their dominance in the league, so they continue to profit from a vicious cycle of winning that excludes other clubs from ever winning. Great teams such as Hamburg, Kaiserslautern or Werder Bremen are shadows of the teams they were decades ago. And in England, a wonderful phenomenon like Nottingham Forest, the European double champions of 1979 and 1980 from the second division, would be impossible today. We could have seen it again with Leicester after they miraculously won the English Premier League, but in the UEFA Champions League they didn't stand a chance. If nothing changes, the winners will be the same for many years to come.

Nowadays, I am more than a simple supporter. I had been connected to professional football as a scout and represented Sporting Kansas City (USA) for more than three and a half years. I was proud to be part of a club in MLS, which is based on a system that fosters equality and the integration of new teams in a planned and well-structured way. Each time a new team enters the competition, they benefit, for example, from the option to choose four players from the existing teams. And that's why a team can win the league in just their second season – and Atlanta United did just that! There is also a salary cap that is regulated and promotes equality. Due to their location, there are teams that have an advantage, such as New York, Toronto (Canada) or Los Angeles, cities that can attract bigger names with more experience, such as Ibrahimovic, Giovinco or David Villa. But the organisation of the league does not allow these teams to become dominant. If that happened, almost every season we would have a final between a team from New York and one from Los Angeles. Teams from mainland USA, such as SKC or Real Salt Lake or Colorado Rapids, would face real difficulties and would end up disappearing. But, fortunately, MLS is a fair system that allows these teams to go for victory in the championship, which SKC managed to do in 2013.

I would like to emphasise my view by quoting the amazing Bobby Robson:

> 'What is a club in any case? Not the buildings or the directors or the people who are paid to represent it. It's not the television contracts, get-out clauses, marketing departments or executive boxes. It's the noise, the passion, the feeling of

belonging, the pride in your city. It's a small boy clambering up stadium steps for the very first time, gripping his father's hand, gawping at that hallowed stretch of turf beneath him and, without being able to do a thing about it, falling in love.'

The question is: Why is this passion limited to only a few teams? Are there different levels of fans in Europe? Is money more important than the core values that should be the basis of any society, such as equal rights? I want to see the Champions League won by any team from any UEFA country. The opportunity to win should not be exclusively for the elite teams. Would it be so difficult to make this a possibility?

I must be honest and say that football has made my life better, but I ask myself what have I given back to football? Well, I can say that football is a type of entertainment, and as a scout if I spot good players they will improve the quality of this entertainment. But I still think I owe football a lot.

There are coaches who have a positive approach to the game in tactical terms. They want to win, but also want to play well, giving their fans great games to watch. But there are others who just want the result, and if they need to just defend, and have a cynical tactical approach to the game to get the result, they will do just that. It's legal and it's acceptable, but for me I don't think the same way about a team that wins 1-0, creating just one chance to score in 90 minutes, versus a team that wins 4-3 and produces more than 20 clear chances to score. A coach is responsible for creating a strategy to win a game, but he can do it by working out the best way to score more goals than the other team instead of conceding fewer. It's quite simple, but it's true. It's disappointing to see coaches with the best players take a defensive approach. A coach who can implement an attacking model with attractive football is an artist, in my opinion. I really mean it, because seeing beautiful football is like watching a piece of art. We shouldn't forget that the key to winning is to find a balance. The most successful teams in football history are the ones in which the coach found balance. A recent example is the French World Cup team from 2018. Coach Didier Deschamps did a great job putting his best players in their favourite positions. He also managed the players' egos, which is also key to finding mental balance within the team. Paul Pogba played so well for France after not performing well at club level for Manchester United in the previous season. I think José Mourinho is a great coach, but I can't see any other reason why Pogba didn't perform than the coach not doing a good job, and I think that must have been a key factor in his sacking from the club. José was great at FC Porto, Chelsea and Inter Milan because he found a perfect match in all aspects that are key to winning: from the tactical balance to ego management, but he failed to do it at Manchester United.

Something that really doesn't make sense in football is watching some coaches or players (or scouts or any other member of staff) get better jobs in better clubs after not working consistently well and failing in their previous ones. I think it's great when a club gives a young player or coach a chance – he can then choose to grab it or not. But what I can't stand is coaches or players continually failing, then still getting another chance in another club, while others who did a good job struggle to stay in the game. I believe that the results and performances should be more important than any other factor. I know coaches who have failed four or five times in a row, and they keep getting good jobs! How is this possible?

I am proud to say that recently a player who SKC tried to sign told me I was 'one of the best people' he'd met in football, and he told me that on a very difficult day for him. He had been told that he wouldn't be starting in a really important match because the coach thought he was about to leave for SKC. When he contacted me, I was expecting him to be angry with me because I had recommended him and built his hopes up, but the decision from our coaching staff had not gone his way. His words were important to me and we need good people in football.

Through writing this book, I have learned a lot about myself. If someone asked me how I would describe myself in terms of how I could add value to a football club, I would say that I am someone who can understand and adapt quickly to different situations or environments and create a strategic plan to help maximise the club's chances of winning as quickly as possible, within the job that I have.

23

INTROSPECTION

Throughout my life, I have always searched for inspiration from other people. I think this is a natural thing to do, particularly when you are younger, and I was lucky to find rich sources of inspiration in different areas, from sports to music and, of course, family and friends. I always try to learn from my mistakes, but also from the mistakes I see other people make.

When I consider my principles and personality, I have to say that I like the way I am. I know I have some characteristics that could be considered as flaws, and they are not ideal, but I wouldn't change any of them. I am very competitive, and I always like to win any competition I am in. I can react badly to defeat, but it's something that I think drives me to future victories and I always maintain my moral standards by playing by the rules.

I realised in my teenage years that I was different from other kids my age in terms of what made me happy. For them, going out at night and dancing at the local disco was enough to make them happy. When I went to college, people were the same. Sometimes I would go out at night with my classmates, but I was kidding myself that I enjoyed it. In my first year at college I felt alone and unhappy. I needed to be in a loving relationship for my life to make sense. At high school I always put my studies first, but at 18 years old I needed someone to make me feel complete. Then in my second year of college I met my future wife Patricia, and a new chapter in my life began. Most people don't know the story of how we met, but it was after I had organised a tribute chatroom to Freddie Mercury on the seventh anniversary of his death (24 November 1998). Patricia registered and entered the chatroom I had set up. We chatted a bit and found that we had more in common than just Queen and Freddie Mercury – we were also at the same college studying economics! She was still in her first year so that's why we hadn't seen each other before. We met face to face three days later and went on a few dates, and we have been together since March 1999. We have been together for nearly 20 years, including almost 11 years of happy marriage. Sometimes we say that it was Freddie who brought us together! It was an amazing coincidence and it has brought us so much happiness. And now, I not only have Patricia but also Leonardo. When he was born another chapter of my life began. The first years were difficult, but the rewards for being a father are much greater than what you give. We didn't become parents until we were 34 because we hesitated, not knowing if we could give Leonardo everything he needed to live a good life. If we could turn back time, we probably wouldn't have delayed it so much.

Everybody should take a look at their own life from time to time. Looking at my life so far, I can't complain at all. I like who I am today, and I have enjoyed my journey so far. I am in a good position to accomplish my short-term goals.

I read a quote once that had a huge impact on me, along the lines of, 'feeling happy is not a natural state of mind for a human being'. I agree. We have our moments of happiness, but most of the time we have to face problems and fight to solve them. Before we achieve a goal that makes us happy, we will probably have spent much more time trying to figure out how to achieve it than the amount of time we are actually happy from it. But, I can say that finishing this book and knowing that it will be published is something that will give me happiness. I have spent a good amount of time working on it, hoping that it will make someone happy after reading it. If I achieve that, I will be able to say that the time and energy I spent on it were worthwhile!

ACKNOWLEDGEMENTS

This book probably wouldn't have happened without the following people:

- The people who gave me opportunities in scouting in the real football world: **Pedro Bessa** was the person who believed in me and opened the door for me at my first club Estoril in 2013; **Kerry Zavagnin** didn't ignore my message and helped me to get a job with Sporting Kansas City in 2015 that consolidated my career and made me grow as a scout; **Radoslaw Kucharski**, a person who shares my vision about the importance of scouting and trusted me to help Legia Warsaw. I owe a special thanks to them and they will always be part of my life.

- The people who introduced me to football in my childhood: **'Zé Manel'** – a neighbour of my grandparents, who influenced me in my early years and helped me to discover football and fall in love with the game – and with SL Benfica! **Grandfather Adão** – I remember the great and funny conversations I had with my late grandfather, who was a Sporting CP supporter. His passion for football was a good influence.

- The people who talk football with me every time I need to and are great company when watching a match: **Bruno** – my childhood friend who has always been by my side during my fantasy football wins and defeats, and enthusiastically supported the clubs I have worked for as a scout! **Rui Viegas** – a friend who is always available to talk about football and give me his views on a player if I need it for my scouting work. I respect his opinions and we have built a solid friendship; **Lopes and Fernando** – these two guys are extraordinary company to watch their beloved club Sporting CP with; both have great enthusiasm and valuable knowledge of the game.

- The people who I can always count on to ease my football frustrations: **Paulo Teixeira** – the first agent I was introduced to and a person who is always available to listen to my frustrations when a player I recommend is not signed and can give you good advice and a man who has enormous experience and knowledge of football. **Darren** – the best friend I have from my fantasy football days! He has a big heart and irreproachable integrity, and he helped me a lot when I suffered my worst fantasy football defeat in 2009. **Flávio** – my manager at my full-time job. He is a great

football lover who is always ready for a good
conversation and never refuses to let me adjust
my work schedule if I have a scouting mission
or an important match, or if I am sad when
my club loses.

I also have to thank the following people, who are important
to me: Hugo, Fátima, Sónia, Claúdia, Paula, Armindo, João,
Manuela, Aunt Célia, Andy, António, Carlos F, Carlos D,
Johan, Terry and the late Milan.

And, of course, thanks to the people who are part of my
life every day: my mother (Judite) and father (Carlos); my
brother (Sérgio); my grandmothers (Joana and Palmira); my
in-laws (José and Céu); and last, but not least, thanks to my
two pillars of strength and the two most important people
in my life: my wife Patricia and my son Leonardo – they are
the real loves of my life!